The Foundations
of American
Constitutionalism

BY ANDREW C. MCLAUGHLIN

WITH AN INTRODUCTION BY
HENRY STEELE COMMAGER

GLOUCESTER, MASS.

PETER SMITH

1972

Table of Contents

Introduction

IT IS CUSTOMARY, even fashionable, to disparage American political thought: after all, America has contributed little to formal political philosophy and boasts few political philosophers. Yet it is no exaggeration to say that over a period of a century and three quarters American politics have been more mature and American political achievements more substantial than those of any other modern people. The contrast here between theory and practice is not really paradoxical, for in a very real sense the apparent bankruptcy of political theory is a product of the obvious prosperity of political practice.

The generation that fought the Revolution and made the Constitution was politically the most inventive, constructive and creative in modern history. Its signal achievement—an achievement whose magnitude grows upon us with the passing of time—was to institutionalize principles and theories that had long been entertained by historians and philosophers, but practiced rarely by statesmen and never by kings. Thus the Americans took the principle that men make government and institutionalized it into the constitutional convention—a mechanism which perfectly satisfied every logical requirement of that philosophical mandate. Thus they took the principle that government is limited by the laws of Nature and Nature's God, and institutionalized it into written constitutions, the separation of powers, and a complex system of checks and balances. They embraced the ancient doctrine of the supremacy of the Law, and institutionalized it in the practice of judicial review. They adopted the notion that sovereignty could in fact be divided and governmental authority distributed, and institutionalized it into federalism. They accepted the theory of

vii

equality—a theory that had never been accorded more than philosophical lip-service—and institutionalized it into a series of social and economic and cultural practices designed to create—almost to guarantee—a classless society. And finally they managed to do what had not been done before—they took the principle of nationalism itself, and actually "brought forth a new nation;" they were the first people to do this.

It is this creative aspect of the American Revolution that Professor McLaughlin celebrates in these luminous and cogent essays. "To teach . . . that the heroes of the Revolutionary controversy were only those taking part in tea parties and various acts of violence is to inculcate the belief that liberty and justice rest in the main upon lawless force," he observes, and insistently directs our attention rather to the study, the legislative chamber and the council room. The Revolution shattered an Empire, to be sure, but it created one, too; it repudiated eighteenth-century English political practices, but vindicated those of the seventeenth century; it rejected current English political institutions, but established American ones in their place. It was, above all, a constructive revolution.

Yet if Americans did not invent political theories, neither did they wholly invent their political contrivances. Where, then, did the institutions come from—the institutions that Americans fabricated during the Revolutionary generation? We take them for granted, McLaughlin says, "as if constitutions, civic order, courts and legislatures, national union and a sentiment of national patriotism, all came into existence quite easily, and without the expenditure of effort or the exercise of wisdom." But revolutions in our own day—most of them barren of political or other contributions—admonish us that we should not. How to explain the American political achievement—the crystallization, in a single generation, of four or five of the most valuable institutions of modern politics? The explanation is to be found in English history, chiefly seventeenth century; as McLaughlin says, in our history we never get too far from the seventeenth century. It is an old story, this, that the American Revolution re-asserted in the New World political principles that the English had asserted during the Puritan Revolution, and then repudiated or abandoned. But it is by no means the whole of the story. Some of the foundations of American constitutionalism—federalism, for example—were products of eighteenth-century British experience; some of them—the new colonial system embodied in the Northwest Ordinance, for instance—were almost wholly American, owed little to the mother country, and almost everything to the circumstances of the New World. What is fascinating is how little our American institutions owe either to political theory, or—notwithstanding the historical and classical window-dressing of so many of the Founding Fathers—to the experience of other peoples, ancient or modern.

It is thirty years, now, since Professor McLaughlin delivered the lectures which make up this volume. What he said then was, for the most part, fresh and original, the quintessence of a lifetime of research and reflection. Much of it, now, is familiar, and even obvious, for like other great scholars, McLaughlin is in danger of being buried beneath the ruins of his own triumph. His achievement was a signal one. In an age that looked with cynical detachment on much of the work of the Founding Fathers, McLaughlin celebrated their positive and enduring accomplishments—accomplishments that seem ever more remarkable as we witness nation after nation foundering in confusion or anarchy. In an age when a large part of the historical fraternity embraced with uncritical enthusiasm the economic interpretations propounded by Charles A. Beard, McLaughlin saw that an economic interpretation was not a conclusion but merely a point of departure. In an age when it was popular to interpret the Constitution as a conservative reaction from the Declaration of Independence and the Revolution itself, McLaughlin saw that the whole era had unity and coherence and that the Constitution represented not a reaction but an advance. In an age that preferred a nationalist to an historical, a revolutionary to an evolutionary interpretation of history, McLaughlin insisted on the continuity of American political institutions.

No scholar of his generation did more—through his teachings, his voluminous writings, his editorship of the *American Historical Review* and of the publications of the Carnegie Institution for Historical Research—to make clear to the American people the true nature of their constitutional system and their political institutions, than did Andrew Cunningham McLaughlin. His contributions to the old "American Nation" series—*Confederation and Constitution*—is the classic description of the critical period; his magisterial *Constitutional History of the United States* remains, after a generation, the most penetrating of all general surveys of our constitutional development. His essays on the courts and on federalism still have the power to inspire fresh research and new interpretations.

To the construction of *The Foundations of American Constitutionalism* McLaughlin brought not only a lifetime of research but a mind singularly judicious and reflective. The essays themselves flow along with such effortless ease that only scholars realize how many original insights, how many seminal ideas, are lodged in them. They are to constitutional history what Turner's essays on the frontier are to the history of the West—and, like Turner's essays, they really encompass the whole of our history. They illuminate not only the Foundations, but the growth and development of our constitutional system, and of our national character as well.

HENRY STEELE COMMAGER

Preface

THE LECTURES HERE appearing in print were delivered at New York University in the spring of 1932 on the Anson G. Phelps Lectureship. The founder of this lectureship desired to provide for a course of public lectures "upon the early history of America, particularly with reference to New England, with the purpose of inculcating a knowledge of the principles which animated the Puritan Fathers and early colonists; and of the influence they have exerted upon modern civilization." This purpose I have attempted to carry out with directness and distinctness. It may seem to the reader—if there be one—that I have neglected to take into proper consideration many influences beside those of the Puritans; but such reflections will not be justified, I think, if the field and purpose of the lectureship be taken into account.

I have adhered in this volume to the lecture form of address and have not changed to the essay form. For this reason, and probably also because of my experiences in nearly half a century of teaching, I have allowed myself to indulge in emphasis and repetition, the common and useful devices of the class-room. My hope is that these characteristics will not be unwelcome in the printed page.

To what extent the contents of the volume are new and of value to the serious student of the period covered, it is impossible for me to say. I am inclined to think that the lectures have some novelty and usefulness because they bring out the relationship between political philosophy and constitutional achievement; and the very emphasis to which I have just referred may be valuable; it is customarily difficult for a reader or a student to find his way through a tangle of historical events if there is no thread leading him to his goal. One can, moreover, never go far astray in insisting upon the connection between the principles and problems of comparatively recent times and those of earlier centuries. In other words, there is likely to be some usefulness in setting forth our indebtedness to the past, if we would know the institutions by which we are encompassed. There can be no harm in teaching constitutional principles historically; for it is time we learned, if we have not as yet, that institutions and principles do not spring full armed from the high brows of Jovian Fathers and are not born from the foam of the sea.

Some of the principles and the historical data which are presented in these lectures have been embodied in previous books and articles which I have written; but the lectures deal chiefly with certain aspects of the matters discussed in earlier studies, and in doing so treat them with much greater detail and, as a rule, with more abundant evidence.

A. C. McL.

Chicago,
September 15, 1932

I

The Church and the Covenant; The Pilgrims; The Plantation Covenants

MY PURPOSE IN these lectures is to trace briefly the historical origins of some of the fundamental and elementary principles of the American constitutional system. In doing this I shall emphasize the influence of New England ideas and principles. Such emphasis will probably not result in distortion of historical facts for certainly in many ways the New Englander was peculiarly conscious of certain theories, and he especially represented those doctrines of the seventeenth century which we find of leading importance in the later days when our institutions were taking formal shape in national and state constitutions. I shall have occasion at first to call your attention to the church polity of advanced Puritanism and to refer also, though briefly, to Puritan theology. It is not, of course, my intention to advocate or to defend the system of either theology or church organization, but to treat them historically and to assign to them such influence as appears justified by facts.

For the first hour or two I shall be chiefly engaged in presenting the ecclesiastical beginnings and also the industrial or economic systems and practices which are important to us if we wish to understand the sources of our institutions. We all know that no understanding of our constitutional system can be quite complete unless we have examined the developments of English constitutionalism and in any such examination we find ourselves being carried back far into history. But it is not my purpose to trouble you with such a survey or to discuss the remoter sources of English and American political theories. My purpose, rather, is to dwell, as I have suggested, on religious and economic practices and doctrines, and, for the time at least, to ignore the influence of British political institutions and law. Let us acknowledge at the outset that those political influences were important, and let us admit the desirability of starting as far back as Magna Carta; after making this concession, we may without misgiving begin our study with the later sixteenth century and look at the beginnings of Puritanism and the appearance of certain elementary ideas in the years immediately before American colonization began.

The Puritanic opposition to the formalities and the ritual which Anglicanism had inherited from Rome is of significance; but of much greater consequence was the belief which grew apace that the Bible and its teachings were sufficient unto life and an ample guide to salvation; and, furthermore, that the proper ecclesiastical system, the form and organization of the church, could be ascertained from the scriptures. It was a movement of significance when Cartwright of Cambridge, if we may select one prominent advocate of reform, declared unlawful all forms of church government save that of the Apostles. Cartwright lost his position and took refuge in Holland in 1570, where liberal-minded men could find refuge. But he soon returned to take active part in the controversies of the time. Certain Puritan ministers were active in their attack upon episcopacy and in their advocacy of an ecclesiastical system founded on scripture. "We believe," said one pronouncement of faith, "the word of God, contained in the Old and New Testament, to be a perfect rule of faith and manners; that it ought to be read and known by all people, and that the authority of it exceeds all authority, not of the Pope only, but of the Church also; and of councils, fathers, men, and angels. We condemn, as a tyrannous yoke whatsoever men have set up of their own invention, to make articles of faith, and the binding of men's consciences by their laws and institutions." Not authority of human rulers or ecclesiastics, not historical tradition, but the written word alone, which was held to be the word of God the Sovereign, was the basis of faith and the source of knowledge.

This was obviously a revolutionary doctrine—revolutionary because it attacked established tradition and because it challenged governmental authority; and it has meaning for us because it rested its case on the interpretation and the application of written documents. To what extent the theory involved or helped to produce the right of individual judgment, the right of each man without molestation to gain from the scriptures for himself his own rules of conduct and to determine for himself the church system with which he wished to be associated, we need not consider; I do not intend to enter upon the question of religious toleration. The influence of the scriptures and the fact that they were examined and commented upon, that on the basis of such examination there arose a marvellous system of theology, the mazes of which could be traversed only by the learned—these things are of primary importance for us. However much we may learn from the history of English liberty in the century preceding the Reformation, and however strongly we may stress the emergence and development of English Parliamentary institutions, such facts cannot entirely overshadow the Non-conformist movement of the later sixteenth and early seventeenth century. Again let me remind you it is not my intention to praise these theories, even though we may find in them one of the main roots of American constitutionalism. The fact is that the New England colonies were founded by men who, without a shadow of turning, believed in the scriptures, in the written word, the direct and imperative mandate of the Most High.

We may turn now to a consideration of extreme Non-conformity, the beginnings of Separatism, the belief that a group of men and women could, without orders from above, establish their own church, and worship without molestation. Probably at the beginning there was no highly developed theory; a few men and women, filled with religious longings and not satisfied with the ceremonies of the establishment, appear to have gathered here and there for

unauthorized worship. Early in the reign of Elizabeth, the authorities of London broke up such an
assembly that met in Plumbers' Hall. Some of these
people were thrust into prison: they believed the
practices of the state church to be wrong and believed they had the right and duty to form a congregation where they might worship in accord with their
own consciences. This, perhaps, may be considered
the beginning of Separatism, but its connection with
later movements cannot be traced with assurance; it
may have been only an isolated or sporadic movement, or only one of the natural and logical products
of Non-conformity and the theory that forms of
worship not connected with scripture were false and
unlawful in the eyes of God.

Now to you and me, or to most of us, the fact
difficult to appreciate is that there should be anything dangerous or abnormal in the idea that men of
their own accord and without official direction can
form a church. Many of the most important principles of modern life are those we take for granted and
do not question; we accept them as if they had always been recognized. Three centuries and a half ago
the temerity of simple men asserting they could form
a church, appeared nothing less than preposterous;
and this attitude of mind was, doubtless, not confined
to functionaries of the establishment and the officials
of the state. Only a few decades earlier, there had
been one church for the whole of western Europe;
the head of the church was powerful, the most conspicuous and awe-inspiring person in Europe. The
universal church in its splendor, its pomp, its wealth,
its beautiful temples of worship, its vast and elaborate hierarchy, in everything, indeed, which arouses
the admiration, appeals to the emotion, and inspires
awe and reverence, excelled the dignity, wealth, and
powers of emperors and kings. It was founded not
on temporal authority but on the basis of divine decree; its papal hand held the keys to heaven. The
ecclesiastical régime of Elizabeth was only less magnificent and powerful within the realm of England
than the older system had been before the break with
Rome. It is not our intention to question the validity

of this conception of the church; but only by pictur-
ing to ourselves the splendor and the power of the
papal church can we appreciate the significance of
the attempt of a few humble folk in the purlieus of
London, simple tradesmen, cobblers, artisans and
craftsmen, to form a church. We may think of our
own reflections if a group of unknown men and
women, rustics or laborers, should assert to-day that
they could form an empire and go along day by day
with no reference to the authority of the state or
nation. The parallel is not exact, but it may help us
to realize how preposterous, how ridiculous, how dis-
turbing it was in the days of Queen Elizabeth to find
men assuming that they could form a church. And
in this way we can see how salient a fact in history
is this event, which we might thoughtlessly pass by
as a matter of no consequence.

Perhaps the group of worshippers of whom we
have spoken and whose leaders were thrust into prison did not in so many words call themselves a
church, though they seem to have chosen their minister and probably to have adopted the principles of
Congregationalism.[1] But not far from this time we
find the beginnings of Separatism, as a distinct system, elaborately presented and defended. The Non-
conformist Puritans desired reform in the established
system; they wished to alter and to simplify it, its
rituals and its ceremonies; they wanted to see it—
there were degrees and differences in their ranks—
brought into conformity with their ideas of the plain
dictates of the Bible. The Separatists were prepared
to create a new system, independent and self-suffi-
cient.

The founder of Separatism was Robert Browne—
"Troublechurch Browne" he came to be called.
He had studied at Cambridge and in all probability
had come under the influence of Cartwright; at all
events, in various fundamentals he was in accord
with that great leader. He prepared to go farther and
to assert boldly the principles of separation of church
and state and the independent right of a body of believers to establish themselves as a church free from

[1] W. Walker, **Creeds and Platforms**, 7.

all interference by temporal authority. It was at
Norwich in Norfolk that Browne worked out his
scheme of church organization and the simpler elements of Congregationalism. This land of East
Anglia was to play a leading rôle in the Puritan
movement in religion and politics. There were many
Dutchmen in the region—not less, it is said, than
30,000 Dutchmen were exiles on English soil; and
about the time when Browne began his work, a majority of the people of Norwich had come from the
Low Countries. And this leads one to think that
Browne was strongly influenced by the Dutch Anabaptists, though of such influence his writings give
no positive evidence.[2] This matter of source or influence is, however, of comparatively little consequence. Browne went to Holland and there published
two books—*A Booke which Sheweth the life and
manners of all true Christians, and howe unlike they
are unto Turkes and Papistes and Heathen folke;*
and *A Treatise of Reformation without tarying for
ainie, and of the wickednesse of those Preachers
which will not reforme till the Magistrate commande
or compell them.*

Certain principles set forth in these volumes are
of importance, and it is because of these principles
or assertions that I have been engaged in this long
introduction which may seem to deal overmuch with
churchly affairs and have little or nothing to do with
the constitutional theories that are to form the core
of my discussion. In the *Booke which Sheweth,*
Browne defines a church: "The church planted or
gathered is a companie or number of Christians or
beleevers, which by a willing covenant made with
their God, are under the government of God and
Christ, and kepe his lawes in one holie communion."
"Howe must the churche be first planted and gathered under one kinde of government? First, by a
covenant and condicion made on God's behalf. Sec-
ondlie, by a covenant and condicion made on our
behalfe.Thirdly, by using the sacrament of Baptisme

2 "Browne's candid spiritual autobiography gives no hint of such
indebtedness, and he mentions no Dutch names among his support-
ers. It is safe to affirm that he had no conscious indebtedness **to**
the Anabaptists." Ibid., 16.

to seale those condicions and covenantes." He believed and taught the separation of the church from the state—the magistrates being able to "doe nothing concerning the Church, but onelie civile, and as civile Magistrates; that is, they have not that authoritie over the church, as to be Prophetes or Priestes, or spirituall Kings, as they are Magistrates over the same: but onelie to rule the common wealth in all outwarde Justice, to maintaine the right welfare and honor thereof with outwarde power, bodily punishment and civill forcing of me [n]. And therefore also because the church is in a common wealth, it is of their charge: that is concerning the outward provision and outward Justice, they are to looke to it; but to compell religion, to plant churches by power, and to force a submission to Ecclesiasticall governement by lawes and penalties, belongeth not them."[3]

We find, therefore, fundamental principles plainly stated: the separation of the church and state; the independent gathering of a few believers into a self-governing body relying upon the scriptures as their guide; the covenant with God to abide by his laws and follow in his ways. When his church was formed at Norwich, he says, "A covenant was made and their mutual consent was given to hold together. There were certain points proved unto them by the scriptures, all which being particularly rehearsed unto them with exhortation, they agreed upon them and pronounced their agreement to each thing particularly, saying: to this we give our consent."[4]

Extended comment on these words may be postponed for the moment. But the word "covenant" and its significance will appear over and over again as we trace the development of American constitutional theory. I need make no apology for the emphasis upon certain words and ideas, for their full bearing in American history is, I think, as a rule not fully recognized. I therefore allow myself space for a few illustrations of this idea that a church could be formed by covenant, or by a series of covenants, that

---

[3] H. M. Dexter, **Congregationalism . . . as Seen in Its Literature,** 101-5.

[4] Ibid., 105. Spelling of the original is here modernized.

is to say, by promises and agreements and reciprocal conditions. In 1593, one Daniel Buck deposed that, when he was united to the church, he made protestation that he would walk with the rest of the congregation so long as they did walk in the way of the Lord and so far as might be warranted by the word of God. In 1616, we find that the people forming a church, standing together, joined hands, and solemnly covenanted with one another in the presence of Almighty God, "to walk together in all Gods ways and ordinances, according as he had already revealed, or should further make them known to them."[5] Robinson, the great and able leader of those Separatists who were immediately connected with the Pilgrims who came to America in 1620, thus describes a church: "A company consisting though but of two or three separated from the world, whither unchristian, or antichristian, and gathered into the name of Christ by a covenant made to walk in all the wayes of God knowen unto them, is a Church, and so hath the whole power of Christ."[6]

We are not engaged now primarily in the history of religion or church polity; and so, though it is by no means an unimportant fact that to the present day the Congregational churches rest on a covenant freely entered into by their members, I am simply stressing at this moment the one fact, that, three hundred years and more ago and from that day to this, the idea of a covenant or contractual relationship was the central and pivotal idea in the organization of a church. Where Congregationalism or Separatism or Independency went, there went also the theory and the fact of compact and convenant.

We have now reached a pivotal position, which everyone can see is germane to the main theme of my lectures. The central idea of Separatism was not— at least it is not for us just now—the distinction between the church and the state; it is not so much the belief that the state should not interfere with the church (very important though that principle may be), as the corollary of that assertion—that

[5] Ibid., 378 n.
[6] Ibid., 393.

people can establish their own church by coming together and entering into a covenant or contract of mutual support. What was fundamental or basic in this idea? First, the assumption of individual existence and of individual right. Whether Browne and the others thought or spoke much of the right of a single person to choose for himself the road to salvation, the underlying philosophical principle was the actual existence of the separate individual man. Second, the individual in agreement with others could form a church, a body that had its own life and being, and, within a certain or uncertain area, its own authority; it had the whole power of Christ. As the result of compact, covenant, and condition, men could form a new relationship and establish a new and real body.

Lest I seem to be dealing only with the thoughts and declarations of a simple folk of three hundred years or more ago, may I anticipate my story by reminding you that the two ideas which have just been stated are salient ideas in the history of popular government and political theory. No one can possibly read with full understanding the constitutional history of the United States, or follow through the discussions and the controversies that form the core of that history, without finding himself confronted constantly with the doctrine of individual liberty and the process of association of individuals into a new and vital whole.

It was inevitable that Browne himself should be led away from the problem of church polity into the field of political speculation. His remarks on this subject are brief, but they illustrate the natural tendency to extend one's theories beyond the field of one's immediate interest. He gave definitions "so generall that they may be applied also to the civill State." "What agreement must there be of men?" he asks. "For church governors there must be an agreement of the church. For civil magistrates, there must be an agreement of the people or Common welth." "The agreement also for the calling of civill Magistrates should be like unto this, excepting their Pompe and outward power, and orders established meete for the people."[6A] We thus find Browne—this obscure preacher and troublemaker—laying down principles of very broad scope and application; but if they appeared only in his pamphlets and his preaching, they would not challenge our attention. We are interested in them because they were early pronouncements of what came to be a widely accepted theory of political and social relationship, and they certainly were of the utmost importance, as I will seek to point out to you, in the upbuilding of the New England colonies and in the development of the processes and principles of later political systems.

It would be going too far to assert the intention of Browne or his fellow associates to establish democratic government or the democratic state. In fact the word "democracy" I am intentionally avoiding, because the term has so many implications and connotations. But he did hold that all rightful authority came from the command of God and the agreement of men. "His picture of the covenant-relation of men in the church, under the immediate sovereignty of God, he extended to the state; and it led him as directly, and probably as unintentionally, to democracy in the one field as in the other. His theory implied that all governors should rule by the will of the governed, and made the basis of the state on its human side essentially a compact."[7]

My desire is not to leave you with the impression that we are dealing with an isolated phenomenon of no general importance or only an episode in the history of denominationalism. The words of Browne, generally considered the founder of Separatism, or Independency, or Congregationalism—the sect of these simple folk called Brownists in the earlier days—have been quoted here partly because in simple terms they announce pivotal ideas of ecclesiastical and political order. If the ideas were only isolated and unprovocative, without meaning in the

[6A] Cf. Charles Borgeaud, **The Rise of Modern Democracy in Old and New England,** 34.

[7] Williston Walker: **Creeds and Platforms of Congregationalism,** 15.

general history of political theory, they would, it is true, be of historical interest because they were the foundation of the Pilgrim Church and, largely, of the Puritan Church of Massachusetts Bay. But my main purpose here is to point out that the Brownists not only asserted certain theories; they acted upon them. Those theories were essentially theories of social compact, that system of political philosophy which had vast influence and wide acceptance for a century and more after Browne and his immediate followers had been laid in their graves.

I am not attempting to declare that Browne originated these political doctrines, that he and his successors were solely responsible for the vogue and influence of these ideas; my purpose is chiefly to show that Brownists and Independents, the Pilgrim Fathers, and others of this faith, actualized and made concrete, though in simple fashion, certain principles which in the course of time were widely accepted and were of enormous influence. The social-compact philosophy, which I shall subsequently discuss and treat with, I fear, tedious detail, is not uncommonly thought of, if thought is bestowed at all, as a philosophical system and as nothing more; it may be interesting to the book-learned as a phase of human thought, which, however, bears no particular application to the realities of life or to the serious processes of history. My purpose is to associate that philosophy with American history and the basis of American constitutional theory.

Some one may justly question the emphasis upon Separatism, because such emphasis neglects other forces and the prevalence of ideas which cannot be associated with these little despised sects. There were other pronouncements. The judicious Hooker, who cannot, of course, be classed with the Brownists or extreme Puritans, gave utterance to some theories that were of great importance; and though the advanced compact-philosophers of the next century did not entirely follow Hooker's reasonings, he had great influence. He said that, to take away the mutual grievances of a state of nature, there was for

men "no way but only by growing into composition
and agreement amongst themselves"; and he declared that, as princes and potentates "naturally have no
full and perfect power to command whole politic
multitudes of men, therefore utterly without our
consent we could in such sort be at no man's com-
mandment living." I must, however, refrain from
any attempt at the present to indicate the various
sources of this idea of agreement and consent as the
basis of authority, though that theory is the main
theme of my discussion; for obvious reasons it is
best for the time being to keep our attention directed
to the Separatists and their actualization of theory.

We need not enter here upon the story of the Pilgrims, eloquently told in Bradford's *History of Plymouth Plantation*. Bradford speaks of their earlier
experiences in England, and how the Lord had
touched their hearts "with heavenly zeale for his
trueth; . . . And as the Lord's free people, joyned
them selves (by a covenant of the Lord) into a
church estate, in the felowship of the Gospell, to
walke in all his wayes, made known, or to be made
known unto them (according to their best endea[v]-
ours whatsoever it should cost them, the Lord assist-
ing them. . . . But after these things; they could not
long continue in any peaceable condition; but were
hunted and persecuted on every side, so as their
former afflictions were but as flea-bitings in compari-
son of these which now came upon them. For some
were taken and clapt up in prison, others had their
houses besett and watcht night and day, and hardly
escaped their hands; and the most were faine to flie
and leave their houses and habitations, and the
means of their livelihood."[8] They fled to Holland
"wher they heard was freedome of Religion for all
men."[9]

How they established themselves there we need
not inquire. Sundry difficulties encompassed them in
their new home. "But that which was more lament-
able, and of all sorowes most heavie to be borne,

    8 Bradford, **History of Plymouth Plantation,** (Mass. Hist. Soc. edi-
tion, 1912), 1, 20, 22, 24.
    9 Ibid., 25.

was that many of their children, by these occasions, and the great licentiousness of youth in that countrie, and the manifold temptations of the place, were drawne away by evill examples into extravagante and dangerous courses, getting the raines off their neks, and departing from their parents."[10] So the decision was reached to migrate to the new world. Negotiations were begun with the Virginia Company of London, which owned a vast territory stretching some four hundred miles along the Atlantic coast. Their intention was to form one of the little semi-independent, or rather self-dependent communities, which the Company was then planning to use in building up Virginia; and it is to be noticed that, had the Pilgrims at last settled within the area owned by the Virginia Company, they would have had, at the beginning at least, considerable control, perhaps practically complete control, of their own affairs.

The prolonged and troublesome negotiations that preceded their migration need not detain us. They finally succeeded in securing the pecuniary means for crossing the ocean and founding their colony. To do this it was necessary to enter into a joint-stock arrangement with certain London merchants, and this connection with mercantile methods was a matter of much importance in the later history and development of their settlement. Later on we shall have occasion to see something of the nature of the joint-stock-system; at this point, two facts need special attention: (1) The Pilgrims were participants in a joint-stock enterprise, that system of coöperative effort which reached its ultimate in the establishment of great trading corporations, a number of which had already been founded for the extension and development of English commerce. (2) Because of this coöperative enterprise and this common business interest, the Pilgrims were necessarily compelled to act coöperatively and at first entirely as a community. This being so, we might possibly assert that business, not religion, held the people together;

[10] Ibid., 55.

that commercial or pecuniary organization, not church fellowship, formed the bond of union and of unity in the primitive state. This, however, is not the whole truth. Both influences need to be taken into consideration: they were a business community and they were a religious community. The influence of the joint-stock scheme and of corporate forms will be spoken of more at length in another lecture. I am asking you now to notice the combination—business and religion, the church and the corporation, the covenant and the joint-stock agreement.

When the voyagers in the bleak days of early winter found themselves far to the north of their expected destination,[11] and outside of the territory of the Virginia Company which had granted them permission to make a settlement and to manage their own affairs, they entered into the famous Mayflower Compact. It was "occasioned partly by the discontented and mutinous speeches that some of the strangers amongst them had let fall from them in the ship; That when they came a shore they would use their owne libertie; for none had the power to command them, the patente they had being for Virginia, and not for New england, which belonged to an other Government, with which the Virginia Corpany had nothing to doe. And partly that shuch an acte by them done (this their condition considered) might be as firme as any patent, and in some respects more sure." The most important sentences of this justly famous document are as follows: "Haveing undertaken, for the glorie of God, and advancement of the Christian faith, and honour of our king and countrie, a voyage to plant the first

[11] There are few passages in literature so skilfully written, so real, so moving, and so impressive, as the description given by Bradford: "And for the season it was winter, and they that know the winters of that cuntrie know them to be sharp and violent, and subjecte to cruell and feirce stormes, deangerous to travill to known places, much more to serch an unknown coast. Besides, what could they see but a hidious and desolate wilderness, full of wild beasts and willd men? and what multitudes ther might be of them they knew not . . . For summer being done, all things stand upon them with a wetherbeaten face; and the whole countrie, full of woods and thickets, represented a wild and savage heiw. If they looked behind them, ther was the mighty ocean which they had passed, and was now as a maine barr and goulfe to separate them from all the civill parts of the world." Bradford, **History of Plymouth Plantation,** (Mass. Hist. Soc. edition, 1912), I, 155-156.

colonie in the Northerne parts of Virginia, doe by
these presents solemnly and mutually in the presence of God, and one of another, covenant and
combine our selves togeather into a civill body politick, for our better ordering and preservation and
furtherance of the ends aforesaid; and by vertue
hearof to enacte, constitute, and frame shuch just
and equall lawes, ordinances, acts, constitutions, and
offices, from time to time, as shall be thought most
meete and convenient for the generall good of the
Colonie, unto which we promise all due submission
and obedience."[12]

The source, nature, and effect of this solemn
agreement have been the subject of much discussion.
We must first notice that, as already stated, the settlers had been given the authority to found a colony
or plantation within the Virginia Company's territory and there to manage their own affairs. That
company had passed, a few months previously, the
following order: "Itt was ordered allso by generall
Consent that such Captaines or leaders of Perticulerr
Plantacons that shall goe there to inhabite by vertue
of their Graunts and Plant themselves their Tennantes
and Servantes in Virginia, shall have liberty till a
forme of Government be here settled for them, As-
sociatinge unto them divers of the gravest and
discreetes of ther Companies, to make Orders, Ordinances and Constitucons for the better orderinge
and dyrectinge of their Servants and buisines provided they be not Repugnant to the Lawes of England." From this we may argue that the colonists
were simply doing for themselves in another region
what they were entitled to do by the permission of
the Virginia Company, and indeed of that fact there
can be no reasonable doubt; and probably they were
influenced by the terms of that permission. But it
is impossible, nevertheless, to neglect the word
"covenant," and not see in the compact the transmutation of a church covenant into the practical
foundation of a self-governing community. It may be
more technically correct to say that in forming the

[12] Ibid., 189-191.

compact they were making use of the same *idea* and
principle as that on which they had built their
church. Now, I am not greatly interested in this act
of the Pilgrim Fathers, as one particular and romantic episode. My chief interest lies in the developing
principle of association of individuals by agreement,
covenant, compact, or contract, into a body, with
power and privilege for self-government. The associating process, and its results, what are they but
the essence of the theory of democracy, as a system of government, and the center of free constitutionalism? And this dramatic action of the Pilgrims
is simply a cardinal example of the principle that we
are examining.

The Mayflower Compact was not in itself very
meaningful, though practically on the basis of this
agreement the settlement was founded; and, supported by a patent which the Pilgrims received from
the Council for New England, a corporation resident
in England and possessing the land, the colony grew
and placidly flourished. Plymouth, however, at no
time had one tithe of the influence of the Puritan
colony established ten years later at Salem and Boston. If the compact were really unique, though dramatic and romantic in its appeal, we might pass it
by with no extended comment. But in fact it was
only the first of a series of plantation covenants,
used by the founders of little towns and communities in New England. The extent and the character
of these agreements can scarcely be overestimated,
if we wish to have clearly and sharply in our minds
the prevalence and the importance of this idea of
agreement or compact—this essential idea of a
community (I use the word community with strict
adherence to its significance) formed by the processes of individual consent.

Here, however, I must break in upon my ruminations concerning the principle of agreement, transfer-
red from the creation of a Separatist church to
become the basis of a government. Later on I shall
consider another form of association containing in
some considerable measure the same elementary idea
—the corporation. Let us content ourselves for the

present with noticing that during the voyage the Pilgrims were organized into a body with officers managing their affairs; and this organization took place without any explicit dependence upon or reference to the patent or express permission of the Virginia Company, which was to take effect upon their landing in Virginia. It was apparently the custom, I know not how widely practiced, for passengers, not the seamen, to form among themselves and for themselves an association for order and self-government during the duration of their voyage. This seemingly was an old and established method, whereby those not immediately subject to the skipper's discipline looked after their own affairs.

This being so, what was the Mayflower Compact but an example of the old "sea law"? What did the Pilgrims do but transmute the system and principle of self-direction, under which they had lived during the weary weeks at sea, into a similar arrangement for their conduct on land? If you argue thus, you may banish *in toto,* as I am not inclined to do, the influence of Separatism, and all sorts of political or religious philosophy; you can direct your attention to the ways and habits of those that went down to the sea in ships. Whatever may be said, the "sea law," in its possible or probable effect, illustrates, as we examine it, the likelihood of many currents of influence, and bids us be on our guard lest we single out one thing—the church covenant, for example—and make its influence not only supreme but complete. Anyone carefully studying history discovers ere long that simplification is likely to distort truth; and, therefore, I wish to remind my hearers that the selection of the church and the covenant as the source of the salient idea that we are searching for ought not to lead us to forget other sources and other influences.

But what was the old "sea law"? There is one very interesting example of the practice. It recounts the method used on board a ship sailing from Riga to Tramünd, only thirty years before the Pilgrims looked out upon the "wetherbeaten" face of the unhospitable New England coast:

"After we had driven half a day under full sail [from Riga], then the Skipper, Bernhard Schultz, of Lübeck called us together according to custom and made the usual speech to us, who were forty-seven all told, to the following purport: 'Seeing that we are now at the mercy of God and the elements, each shall henceforth be held equal to his fellows, without respect of persons. And because, on this voyage, we are in jeopardy of sudden tempests, pirates, monsters of the deep and other perils, therefore we cannot navigate the ship without strict government. Wherefore I do hereby most earnestly warn and instantly beseech every man, all and singular, that we hear first of all a reading of God's word from the Scriptures, both text and notes; and then that we approach God steadfastly with prayer and hymn that He may vouchsafe us fair winds and a prosperous journey. After which we will set about to ordain and establish a government by the most prudent according to the customary sea-laws; which office (as sea-law hath it) no man may refuse to undertake, but must rather be ready to exercise it strictly and without respect of persons, even as each desireth that God may deal with him at his last end and at that dreadful day, truly and without flinching, and with all diligence that may be.' Then followed the preaching and prayers; after which the aforesaid Skipper, by universal consent, chose as our judge or Reeve a noted citizen of Riga, Dietrich Finger by name [here follows a list of other officials]. After which ordinance of our government, then the following sea-laws were read out from the written text, that men might obey them."

The "sea-laws" included a number of declarations as to what "no man" should do, and among them, "No man shall spill or pour away more beer than he can cover with his foot, under penalty of a cask of beer, or less according to the circumstances." When they were within "near half a day's sail of the port of Tramünd, in the territory of Lübeck, then the Keelmaster or Skipper made his reckoning according to custom, after which the Bailiff" resigned the position which he had held and urged that each man should forgive his fellow what ever had passed on shipboard. "If however any yet thinketh that any matter have been unwarrantably judged, let him speak out now when we can yet dispute of that matter; whereunto I for my part will give all possible diligence to settle the dispute, and leave no stone unturned. . . ."[13]

Did the Pilgrims starting on this long voyage across the Atlantic organize in accord with the old sea law, and did they, in effect if not in detail, do just what the passengers of the German ship had done as here described? Of that there can be no reasonable doubt, and though the subject is not of major importance in our attempt to trace out the main lines of development of a constitutional principle, it deserves more than passing attention because it appears to be unknown or at least to be often ignored by the learned commentators upon the history of Massachusetts. Speaking of their preparation for their journey, Bradford says, "All things being now ready, and every bussines dispatched, the company was caled togeather, and this letter read amongst them [a letter of Robinson, which will be referred to later] which had good acceptation with all, and after fruit with many. Then they ordered and distributed their company for either shipe, as they conceived for the best. And chose a Govr. and 2 or 3 assistants for each shipe, to order the people by the way, and see to the dispossing of there provissions, and shuch like affairs. All which was not only with the liking of the maisters of the ships, but according to their desires."[14] Martin, it seems, was the governor of the *Mayflower,* but, apparently, after both companies had been crowded on board the *Mayflower,* Carver was chosen governor.

Immediately after the transcription of the Mayflower Compact, as it is given in Bradford's narrative, we find the statement, "After this they chose, or rather confirmed, Mr. John Carver, (a man godly

[13] **Life on a Hanse Ship,** in G. G. Coulton, **A Mediaeval Garner,** pp. 156-158. The document is extracted from J. C. v. Fichard, **Frankfurtisches Archiv,** 11, 245-246.
[14] Bradford, op. cit., 135, 136.

and well approved amongst them) their Governour for that year."[15] These words "rather confirmed"[16] have occasionally perplexed the historian; but it seems obvious that Carver, chosen as governor under sea law and in accordance with the desire of the skipper, was confirmed in the office, as the Pilgrims were preparing to disembark and begin their tasks on land. What then was the source of the governorship? Almost certainly, the sea agreement; and the governor continued to be the leading official in the succeeding decades. But once more we hesitate; once again there is danger of over-emphasizing one source of influence; for if we scan Bradford's words again, we notice that he speaks of the selection, for the government of the Pilgrim's during the voyage, of a governor and two or three assistants; and those words at once remind us of the corporation, of the great and the small trading companies, whose officers were "governors" and "assistants." The fact is, as we shall see more fully in the next lecture, it seems impossible to keep free from the corporation and its influence on American institutions.

Though we must acknowledge various influences and among them the "sea law" which was the immediate antecedent of the famous Compact, we must remember that the main body of the settlers constituted a church.[17] And, moreover, John Robinson, in his letter to the departing Pilgrims reminded

[15] Bradford, op. cit., 192.

[16] A footnote by the editors of the Massachusetts Historical Society edition of Bradford (1912) says with reference to the confirmation of Carver, "Some confusion has arisen from the insertion of this phrase. Deane (editor of an earlier edition and a man of great learning in all that had to do with early Massachusetts) believes that 'it may possibly be an inadvertence, and may have been intended to apply to his reelection' in 1621. . . . It is also possible that Carver was governor, on the Speedwell, as Martin was on the Mayflower, a place due to him as one of the purchasing agents." This latter supposition seems almost inevitably correct: that when the two companies were united, Carver became governor for the whole, and that when they prepared to disembark he was rechosen to act on land, and in Bradford's mind there was a continuance of the organization under the sea law. Hence the word "confirmed."

[17] "It was also agreed on by mutuall consente and covenante, that those that went should be an absolute church of them selves, as well as those that staid." Bradford, **History of Plymouth Plantation,** (Mass. Hist. Soc. edition, 1912), 1, 98.

them that they are "become a body politik, using amongst your selves civill governments"; he admonished them to choose "shuch persons as doe entirely love and will promote the commone good," and to yield to them all "due honour and obedience."[18]

I have said that this Compact was only the first and the most conspicuous of the plantation covenants, which were framed by settlers in New England when they moved into the wilderness beyond the immediate reach of the colonial government. Without intending to smother you with data to establish my position, I must refer to instances and give a few brief quotations, because it is my purpose to make abundantly clear the doctrine or the theory of compact or covenant which permeated the mind of the American Puritan. The founders of the Bay Colony, though at the beginning not Separatists, soon accepted Separatist principles and practices. But first let us notice the statement of John Winthrop, in a sermon written on board the *Arbella,* the ship which brought the founders of Boston to America: The work we have in hand "is by a mutuall consent, . . . to seeke out a place of cohabitation and Consorteshipp under a due forme of Government both civill and ecclesiasticall . . . Thus stands the cause betweene God and us. We are entered into Covenant with Him for this worke. . . . The Lord hath given us leave to drawe our own articles. . . . Now if the Lord shall please to heare us, and bring us in peace to the place we desire, then hath hee ratified this covenant and sealed our Comission, and will expect a strict performance of the articles contained in it."[19] How clearly this brings out the

<hr/>

[18] John Robinson's letter on the departure of the Pilgrims: "Lastly, whereas you are become a body politik, using amongst your selves civill governments, and are not furnished with any persons of spetiall eminencie above the rest, to be chosen by you into office of government, let your wisdome and godliness appeare, not only in chusing shuch persons as doe entirely love and will promote the commone good, but also in yeelding unto them all due honour and obedience in their lawfull administrations; not behoulding in them the ordinarinesse of their persons, but Gods ordinance for your good, not being like the foolish multitud who more honour the gay coate, then (than) the vertuous minde of the man, or glorious ordinance of the Lord." Ibid., 134.

[19] Massachusetts Historical Society **Collections**, Third Series, VII, 45-46.

essentials of thinking in the terms of contract—contractual and legalistic relationship.[20]

An interesting example of the way in which the idea was applied to civil affairs appears in Rhode Island. The settlers under Roger Williams adopted in 1637 a written covenant whereby they subjected themselves "in active and passive obedience to all such orders and agreements as shall be made for public good of the body in an orderly way, by the major consent of the present inhabitants, masters of families incorporated together in a Towne fellowship, and others which they shall admit unto them, only in civil things."[20A] In the founding of that colony by various groups we find a series of covenants or compacts. Of like character were the agreements drawn up in the earlier settlements of New Hampshire. The Bible was searched, as doubtless it had been many times before, to demonstrate that covenanting was the Lord's chosen method for social and religious combination; and Biblical texts were sought to prove the right and the power in the congregation or the community to choose officers.

Of special interest are the Fundamental Articles of New Haven (1639), which refer to a "plantation covenant" previously made. "This covenant," the

[20] I have made no attempt to present the differences at the beginning of settlement between the Puritans at the North and the Pilgrims of Plymouth. The former were, in general, not Separatists at first. But the adoption of Separatism came speedily. "We, of the congregation," wrote Winthrop, "kept a fast, and chose Mr. Wilson our teacher, and Mr. Nowell an elder, and Mr. Gager and Mr. Aspinwall, deacons. We used imposition of hands, but with this protestation by all, that it was only as a sign of election and confirmation, not of any intent that Mr. Wilson should renounce his ministry he received in England." **Winthrop's Journal** (Hosmer's edition, 1, 51, 52. So careful were they at first not to admit outright that they were separated from the old church. But the influence and the example of the Separatists at Plymouth are demonstrable. From practical necessity and from conscious choice, the Puritans of New England became Separatists. Cf. Herbert L. Osgood, **The American Colonies in the Seventeenth Century**, 1, Part 11, Chap. III, and especially 204-207.

But there was too much of the authoritative policy and theory of Calvinism, and there was too much of the dominating orthodoxy of the more determined leaders to allow each little body of believers to go its own way without guidance or interference. The truth is the religious and political history of Massachusetts in the seventeenth century presents a profoundly interesting example of what, to the uninitiated at least, appears to be the conflict between the salient ideas of Calvin. But my desire is in these pages to keep free from discursive details that I may point out the march of certain prominent principles.

[20A] Ibid., 336.

Articles say, "was called a plantation covenant to distinguish itt from [a] chur. covenant which could nott att thatt time be made, a chur. nott being then gathered, butt was deferred till a chur. might be gathered according to God." By these Articles, which were adopted by a show of hands, the people bound themselves "to esta.[blish] such civill order as might best conduce to the secureing of the purity and peace of the ordina[nces] to themselves and their posterity according to God."[21] Possibly these references and quotations are enough to establish beyond all question the influence of the scriptures, the right which men found in the scriptures by association and covenant to organize a church and civil government, and, in church and temporal community, to choose from among themselves their own ministry and their own governors.

But we cannot pass over unnoticed the organization of the river towns of Connecticut, where, it has been said, was formed the first written constitution in history. The Fundamental Orders of 1638-39, state in the opening paragraph: "And well knowing where a people are gathered togather the word of God requires that to mayntayne the peace and union of such people there should be an orderly and decent Government established according to God, to order and dispose of the affayres of the people at all seasons as occation shall require; doe therefore assotiate and conjoyne our selves to be as one Publike State or Conmonwelth; and doe, for our selves and our Successors and such as shall be adjoyned to us att any tyme hereafter, enter into Combination and Confederation togather, to mayntayne and presearve the liberty and purity of the gospell. . . . As also in our Civill Affaires to be guided and governed according to such Lawes . . . as shall be made. . . ." They thereupon provided for two general assemblies

---

[21] "Then Mr. Davenport declared unto them by the scripture whatt kinde of persons might best be trusted with matters of government, and by sundry arguments from scripture proved that such men as were describ(ed) in Exod. 18. 2. Deut. 1. 13, with Deut. 17. 15, and I Cor. 6: 1 to 7, ought to be intrusted by them, seeing (they) were free to cast themselves into thatt mould and forme of common wealth which appeareth best for them . . ." MacDonald, **Select Charters,** 68-9.

each year, for the election of a Governor and magistrates, for the use of a written ballot, for a nominating system; and in other ways they outlined a fairly comprehensive system of government.

The forms of government which were set up in Connecticut were substantially the same as those which Massachusetts had worked out during the first decade of the colony's life; there was little that was quite original and without precedent; but that fact need not obscure the significance of this process of free association into a commonwealth. The articles thus adopted unquestionably were influenced, if not produced, by the church covenant and the processes by which churches were organized, but they did not have all the qualities of a modern state constitution. Not only were they less elaborate and less precise, but in one respect they did not bear the fundamental character of modern constitutions: they did not operate as a rigid limitation on the power of the general court or assembly. Despite all this, and though much remained to be done before the full theory of the American constitutional system was made actual, there is something especially impressive and especially significant in this association of men into a commonwealth, the processes they followed, and the principles they announced or assumed. It is further to be noticed that Rhode Island and Connecticut later became corporate colonies, the forms of government being similar to those spontaneously adopted, and that these charters continued to be the constitutions of these states for decades after the Revolution.

We have thus found a conspicuous principle of American constitutionalism—we cannot say "beginning," but we can say manifesting itself and obtaining *concrete* expression—in the religious movements and aspirations of the late sixteenth century and early seventeenth century; we have seen in the plantation covenants the theories of Browne carried out; and in a simple way his theories were made applicable to the civil state. I emphasize the word concrete, because, as I have said, I make no assertion that the church covenant or the philosophy of Separatism was the sole source of certain essential principles of profound significance; but the actual realization of certain theories, the finding of objective expression, takes the doctrines out of the rarefied air of philosophical speculation.

II

The Colonial Corporation; Early Institutions; The Beginnings and the Character of American Representation

WE SHALL HAVE to return before long to a further study of contract and compact; but we now turn our attention to a form of association, which had perhaps in some respects more influence than church and religion on the early development of American institutions. One of the great instruments or agencies which have contributed to the development of the British Empire is the trading company or the corporation. Its importance in the process of expansion can scarcely be over-emphasized. I do not mean to assert that in all cases where the corporation actually promoted the political empire, it was consciously established for that express purpose; a large part of the British Empire has been founded almost inadvertently, in a fit of absentmindedness; the government of the greatest colonizing nation the world has ever known was not a colonizing government; commonly, if not always, the beginnings of a colony and its early struggles have been looked upon with little more than languid interest. But it is necessary to think of only such prominent corporations as the East India Company and the Hudson Bay Company, to get an impression of the field and effect of corporate activity. In our own history, we find two especially important corporations, the Virginia Company of London and the Governor and Company of Massachusetts Bay; both of them effective in colonization, both of them influential in the development of American institutions.

The history of the trading corporation, a form of business organization, is therefore of interest to anyone looking for the beginning and the development of American constitutionalism. We cannot here endeavor to seek the origins of the principle or practice of incorporation or to find its distinct antecedents in ancient or mediaeval history. My first interest is in the idea of association, the process whereby individuals can organize a body; the process had been pretty widely followed long before the formation of the Puritan church by covenant and long before the beginnings of American settlement.

We find the beginnings in England of joint-stock enterprises in the latter part of the Middle Ages. There is at least some evidence that there was connection between the little social or religious guilds which flourished in those centuries and the formation of joint-stock companies, which grew to be of such tremendous importance in the development of English trade. And there is also some evidence of the connection between the social guild in the time of Elizabeth on the one hand, and, on the other, the beginnings of Separatism and the establishment of the Brownist congregations.

"The example of the boroughs or municipal corporations, and of the corporations of merchants and artisans, is often quoted in the pamphlets of the early period of Congregationalism. It is well known that both these were the outcome of the Guilds of the Middle Ages, whose internal organization they had borrowed. It is extremely probable that, though the Bible supplied the Separatists with the original idea of their Church covenant, the form which that covenant actually took in their first congregations was not uninfluenced by their knowledge of the statutes established by the founders of these Guilds, and by the custom which then prevailed of requiring new members to give their adhesion to these statutes by an individual vote. So striking are the analogies, that it even seems probable that Brown, when he was organizing his Church at Norwich, had before him, side by side with his Bible, the statutes of one of these pious corporations, once so numerous and influential in the county of Norfolk.

"The larger number had been suppressed little more than thirty years before, in the reigns of Henry VIII. and Edward VI.; but a few had survived, and the most important of those survivors, the famous Guild of St. George, had its headquarters in Norwich. The very name of Company, which was borne by this corporation after the Reformation, was that under which his Church of 'true Christians' presented itself to Brown. It was the only one which the law would at that time sanction."[1]

To establish beyond all question the connection between the joint-stock company and the religious guilds, or to find the connection, if there be such, between the religious guild and the Separatist church, is, however, not a matter of supremest importance. But it is at least interesting to speculate upon the likelihood or the possibility that the associating of individuals into a church and the like associating into a trading-company had the same historical antecedents.[2]

The joint-stock arrangement was simply this: each person adventuring with others in an undertaking for profit, contributed a sum of money; some persons would naturally contribute more than others; with the conclusion of the enterprise, or, if the undertaking was of long duration, at intervals, profits were distributed among the contributors in proportion to their investment. There is no better example

[1] Charles Borgeaud, **The Rise of Modern Democracy in Old and New England,** (1894), 86-7. Borgeaud refers to Toulmin-Smith's **English Gilds,** and says that "Among a hundred statutes of the ancient Gilds of England, . . . forty-six are the statutes of pious foundations in the county of Norfolk, and twelve of these belong to the single town of Norwich, the cradle of Congregationalism."
W. J. Ashley, **An Introduction to English Economic History and Theory,** Pt. II, 136, 138, says, "in the single county of Norfolk, a list which is manifestly imperfect, returns as many as 909 gilds."

[2] "There are features in the first joint-stock ventures that carry one back to the social gild. Such characteristics are of exceptional interest as showing the continuity of the development of associated effort. The continuance of the exclusive spirit, which was necessary only as a bond of union amongst the members, is repeated in the company, not only in the desire for a monopoly, but also in the oath of membership. The terminology of the gild was continued in the naming of the shareholders 'brothers' in the East India company, and in fining those who were absent when summoned to meetings . . ." W. R. Scott, **The Constitution and Finance of English, Scottish, and Irish Joint-Stock Companies to 1720,** I, 152.

of this system than that furnished by the Pilgrims. The joint-stock undertaking was the means adopted for defraying the expenses of the settlement, and it had marked effect upon the development of the colony. By the agreement between the "adventurers"—the London merchants who furnished the money—and the "planters," every person going to America of sixteen years of age or more was rated at £ 10, that sum constituting a single share. If one went in person and contributed £ 10 either in money or provisions, he was counted as having £ 20 in stock, and in the division a double share. The joint-stock organization was to last for seven years, "during which time, all profits and benifits that are gotte by trade, traffick, trucking, working, fishing, or any other means of any person or persons, remaine still in the commone stock untill the division."

For seven years the Pilgrims continued under the joint-stock arrangement, though insuperable difficulties arose in the attempt to carry on faithfully the practice of common toil without personal or individual profit. After the lapse of the seven years, Bradford and the rest took upon their shoulders the task of making repayment to the London adventurers. For over a decade, this task consumed a very large share of the energy, zeal, and interest of the settlers; and business was, of necessity, carried on as a joint or common undertaking. The influence of the commercial forms and practices of the time is not a matter of surmise or speculation, but is perfectly plain.

One of the large trading companies, which indeed might be considered the great-grandfather of them all, bore the title of The Merchants Adventurers. It began in the obscure and unsettled conditions of the Middle Ages; its end was in the nineteenth century.[3] It received several charters from the crown, and in 1564 was fully incorporated. This charter contains those provisions that peculiarly and distinctly describe a corporation; the company was "estab-

[3] W. E. Lingelbach, **The Merchant Adventurers of England, Their Laws and Ordinances with other Documents,** (Philadelphia, 1902), xv.

lished one perpetuall fellowship and comminalty and
body Politick and Corporate"; it was declared to
have "perpetuall succession," and "full lawful and
perfect power . . . in law to sue and impleade to be
sued and impleaded." This charter of incorporation
is of decided interest because of its similarity to the
charters of the companies which in the seventeenth
century engaged in American colonization. In fact
without appreciation of the forms and the activities
of the trading companies some of the characteristics
of early American colonization cannot be understood.

The business affairs of this company were carried
on in large measure outside of England—in the Low
Countries and the nearby regions; it established
what, by only a slight exaggeration or misrepresen-
tation, we may call commercial colonies across the
North Sea. "The 'marte towne' was always a city on
the continent, where the Adventurers resided and
stapled their commodities." Over their membership
and others associated with the enterprise, the company were given extensive authority, so extensive
that it seems at the first glance to have the power and
character of a public rather than a private corporation.

The governor and assistants were entitled to
"exercise full jurisdiction power and authority lawfully to rule and governe the same Fellowship of
Merchants Adventurers of England and their successors and all and every merchant and member of
the same in all their private causes and suits quarrels
and demeanours, offences and complaints amongst
them in the same countries and towns of Holland,
Zealand . . . and to reform decide and pacify all
manner of questions discords and variance, between
themselves and between them or any of them and
other merchants in the said countries . . ."[4] An examination of their ordinances, etc., as "digested into
order" by the secretary in 1608, discloses the astonishing extent of the authority actually exercised

---

[4] Ibid., xv, 233, 234. Lingelbach also maintains that the main
"Government of the Fellowship" was located abroad. Lingelbach,
The Internal Organisation of the Merchant Adventurers of England,
(Philadelphia, 1903), 43.

by the company or its officials.[5] We need to notice
these facts to understand why and how it came about
that some of the early American charters, e.g., the
charter of the Virginia Company of London, contained wide grants of what we should now call governmental or political power.

But the Merchants Adventurers were not the
only company engaged in foreign trade. In the days
of Elizabeth, trading corporations flourished, while
English commerce grew into scarcely less than
world-wide proportions. The Muscovy Company,
the Levant Company, and others were active—
great combinations resembling our modern corporations but possessed of more power. In 1600, the
East India Company was chartered. The trading
companies of the day were prosperous, showing returns which, if coming to the coffers of the modern
corporation, would satisfy the greediest lover of div-
idends.[6] It is not surprising to find that the men who
were interested in establishing Virginia asked for
incorporation. In 1609, the charter of the Virginia
Company of London was issued; the company was
composed of several hundred persons, many of
them conspicuous in the social and commercial life
of the time. It was in the hands of men of rare
vision and of determination from about 1618 to
its dissolution by the crown in 1624; and, though
its life was short, we must ascribe to that corporation some of the more important beginnings of
American institutions.

"In 1619," some writer has declared, "a representative assembly broke out in Virginia." This implies or seems to imply some kind of uprising in the
colony; but, more likely, it indicates that the every-
day son of Britain, wherever he might be, carried in
his system this malady of free representative government. We hear, not infrequently, of the glorious
significance of the transfer of English institutiona-

---

[5] Lingelbach, **The Merchant Adventurers of England, Their Laws
and Ordinances with other Documents,** 1-197.

[6] "The capital employed by the East India Company during the
period from 1609 to January 1613 had yielded a maximum profit
of 234 per cent, and minimum profit of 121-2/3 per cent, not per
annum, but during the period the funds were employed, which was
longer. The Russia company had been remarkably fortunate, and it
was able to pay 90 per cent. annually in 1611 and again in 1612."
W. R. Scott, op. cit., I, 141.

lism, as specially embodied in representation, to the shores of the virgin continent. There cannot, it is true, be anything much more important than the beginning of quasi-popular government; and the meeting of the first assembly in the little church at Jamestown, three hundred years and more ago, has its page of honor in American annals. But, of course, the plain fact is that the assembly was called by the order of a corporation, resident and acting in London. That such order was in part influenced by the practices and habits of corporations, I am inclined to believe, though I know no instance of representation in the ordinary practices of the big trading-companies. This is plain, however: the company was for a time in the hands of a few political philanthropists; they were, as one of the stand-pat commercialists of the time declared, men, "of discourse and contemplation, not of reason and judgment"; they were, that is to say, men who used their minds and were speculating upon the possibilities of freer government. They wished, it appears, not to transfer the English system to America, but to carry out theories of orderly and free government, which had not as yet reached fulfillment in the England of their day. Some of them at least belonged to the body of liberals in politics, who were soon to make serious trouble for the arbitrary and wilful Stuarts.[7]

[7] Data on this subject are presented in Alexander Brown's **Genesis of the United States** and his **First Republic in America**. The statements are more or less gossipy and certainly partisan in character; but from other evidences we may judge or at least surmise that they were essentially correct. They were made or said to be made by one Captain Bargrave, who declared "he was afrayd to discover somethinge which he knew of Sir Edwin Sandys his proceeding in those businesses, both because he was so upheld privately in his courses as also that he had the strength of the Court (the meeting of the company or the company itself) to countenance him in all things, and had so carryed the business that he would be sure to hide all his owne ill actions under the name of the Companye." The deponent also declared, "that by his long acquaintance with him and his wayes he was induced verilie to beleave that there was not any man in the world that carried a more malitious heart to the Government of a Monarchie than Sir Edwin Sandys." Bargrave had heard him say, "That if our God from heaven did constitute and direct a forme of Government it was that of Geneva . . . He telling Captaine Bargrave that his intent was to erect a free state in Virginia . . . And to that intent . . . Sir Edwin Sandys moved my Lord of Canteburye to give leave to the Brownists and Separatists of England to goe thither." Brown's **First Republic,** 529-30. There is something especially interesting in the connection between Sandys and the Pilgrims. See, for example, Bradford's **History of Plymouth Plantation,** (Mass. Hist. Soc. edition, 1912), 70.

They decided, it appears, to give concrete illustration of their philosophic principles. In saying this, I do not mean to assert that even representation was set up with no consideration for its effect on the commercial wellbeing of the colony and the corporation.

As our attention is chiefly directed to New England, this brief statement about the Virginia Company must suffice us. But if we should go into details, we should find further reason for saying that, for our understanding of American institutional beginnings, the processes and the discussions of the Virginia Company of London deserve study. We may also make note in passing that, after the dissolution of the Company in 1624, some four years passed before another assembly was called, this time by royal authority. It was called not because of any philanthropic or philosophic desire to extend representative institutions to the new world, but because Charles wished the consent of the planters to certain arrangements about tobacco, that noxious but profitable weed against which James had already issued his famous *Counterblast*.

The Governor and Company of Massachusetts Bay was established as a corporation in the spring of 1628/29. There is nothing on the face of the charter to indicate that, in essential character or purpose, it was thought to be different from other trading companies. Authority to make and establish "all manner of wholesome and reasonable orders . . . and ordinances" was bestowed upon the company. The officers of the corporation were the customary ones—a governor, deputy governor, and eighteen assistants. These officers correspond to the president, vice-president, and board of directors of a modern corporation; [8] to them was assigned the duty of caring for the general interests of the company; but the main authority was in the members of the corporation who were authorized to meet in "Foure Greate and Generall Courts" each year; at

[8] The word "directors," instead of "assistants," appears to have been first used in the African Company which was chartered in 1618, where provision was made for a governor, a deputy governor, and twelve directors. W. R. Scott, op. eit., I, 151.

the Easter meeting the officers were chosen "for the yeare ensueing."

The Virginia Company had lived out its strenuous and stormy years in London; there it had issued its directions for the management of the colony. But hardly had the Massachusetts Bay Company been established, when the decision was reached to move the seat of the company from Britain to Massachusetts. This is commonly called "the transfer of the charter"; the important fact is that the company, as an organized entity—not all its members, in fact only a small number, but the corporation as a legal person—came to this side of the ocean. The company here, with the charter in its possession, began to carry out the purpose of its founders. For us the cardinal fact is that the charter of the corporation became with some modifications the constitution of the commonwealth.

We need not enter upon any detailed study of the contests or disputes concerning the authority of the governor and the assistants. At the beginning, conditions admitted the exercise of wide authority by these officials, because there were apparently not enough members of the corporation in the colony even to supply the prescribed number of the assistants. [9] And for a time the provisions of the charter were plainly avoided. But if we look through the proceedings of the first ten years of the colony's history, we find the influence of a determination of the few to manage affairs, and this was due to several things, among them the belief of the leaders that they were especially competent to safeguard the interests of the settlement. In modern enterprises there appears not infrequently an inclination among officials of a corporation to wield all available power in order to further the interests of the corporation as a whole, as they conceive those interests, and they seem to forget that they themselves are not the corporation. The ordinary stockholder does not play a conspicous rôle in the modern corporation. This natural tendency, we must conceive, was manifested in the early years

[9] The largest number attending the court of assistants in the earlier years was in September, 1630, when twelve were present.

of Massachusetts. But such ruminations are not for us of immense importance. The fact is that the governor and the assistants did take power into their hands, and they used it. This power was specifically granted by the general court (1630, 1631), but the court at that time was made up of those who were actually members of the court of assistants; and thus we are justified in saying that the assistants, in violation of the charter, seized upon the authority. The records do not show any list of the freemen present except the officials when the significant votes were taken. [10]

The first important step of especial interest to us was the enlargement of the corporation by increase in its membership. New members were admitted; and the qualification set for admission was not, as it would be in a modern corporation, purchase of a share of stock, but membership in a church.[11] This was not a narrowing of the company; legally (though in law the situation was not without difficulties because so few freemen of the company were actually within the colony) the authority was in the company's hands. The land belonged to the company; it was charged with the management of colonial affairs; the company as then constituted might have insisted upon going forward with its meager membership. This qualification for participating in the corporate affairs was a qualification which was supposed to be conducive to one of the main purposes of the colony; and if it seems to the modern reader

[10] The **Records** do say that the crucial proposal of October 19, 1630, "was fully assented unto by the general vote of the people, and erection of hands." That the word "people" meant the settlers in general without reference to membership is difficult to believe, though that is not an uncommon interpretation. It was not at all impossible to assume that, though there were only eight persons listed as present in the records and they were assistants, they voted, as they were in that meeting entitled and bound to do, as members of the general court and were therefore designated as people, while freemen would have been the proper word. This may seem an impossible interpretation; but any other, if not impossible, presents difficulties. It certainly required some courage to ask the "people" to consent to a variation of the terms of the charter, which they were legally not entitled to make.

[11] "And to the end the body of the commons may be preserued of honest and good men, it was likewise ordered and agreed that for time to come noe man shalbe admitted to the freedome of this body polliticke, but such as are members of some of the churches within the lymitts of the same." **Records of the Governor and Company of the Massachusetts Bay in New England,** Boston, 1853. I, 87.

a piece of intolerance, that feeling need not obscure the fact of actual expansion of corporate membership. [12]

But ere long there was discontent. Governor Winthrop was inclined to treat the malcontents with a degree of condescending but fatherly superiority. [13] Some things were done in 1632, which may be considered a recognition of the propriety of allowing those persons beyond the closed boundaries of the little governing body to have a word or two to say; and in this connection we see the beginnings of the notion or idea of representation.[14] But the critical step was taken in 1634, when certain freemen who had been deputed "to meet and consider of such matters as they were to take order in at the same general court" [15] desired a sight of the charter. They found there that the laws should be made by the general court, in other words by the main body of the freemen meeting together. [16] This power did

[12] The word "freeman" as used in the American colonial system had differing significances. In Massachusetts it meant those belonging to fellowship of the corporation. In this connection the terms of admission or qualification for membership in the Merchants Adventurers is of interest. See W. E. Lingelbach, **The Internal Organisation of the Merchant Adventurers of England,** 9-15. He there treats of the "Admissions into the ffellowshippe with Orders Concerninge as well ffreemen as Apprentyces."

[13] Notice should be taken of the assertion of the Watertown people, when levy was made "for the fortifying of the town, . . . that it was not safe to pay moneys after that sort, for fear of bringing themselves and posterity into bondage." Winthrop's account of the instruction and chiding given to the ringleaders of the complainants is rather amusing. Plainly the government as then organized had gone beyond the prescribed terms of the charter. But the chided Watertown leaders appear to have taken reproof quietly. **Winthrop's Journal** (Hosmer's ed.), I, 74, 75. Osgood's discussion of the significance of the meeting is naturally important. H. L. Osgood, **The American Colonies in the Seventeenth Century,** I, 156. His interpretation is that Winthrop meant to declare that the corporation had been raised from the domain of private law into that of public law. Of course Osgood's opinion is one always demanding more than mere respect. I cannot, however, escape the idea that what Winthrop had chiefly in mind was the extensive power of the authority actually granted to the corporation, though that power was then being exercised by a few men who had gone beyond the charter.

[14] **Records,** I, 95.

[15] Winthrop, op. cit., I, 122. These persons or deputies were apparently chosen in accord with the resolution of the court of May 9, 1632. "That there should be two of every plantacion appointed to conferre with the Court about raiseing of a publique stocke."

[16] It is interesting to notice that by the charter of the Merchants Adventurers (1564) the governor and assistants had "full power . . . and authority lawfully to rule and governe the same Fellowship of Merchants Adventurers." The freemen of Massachusetts Bay were not ignorant yokels; some of them may well have known of this charter or other corporate charters and on that account have been uncertain of the extent of power given by the Massachusetts company charter to the governor and assistants.

not rightfully and legally belong to the governor and assistants. In an eventful meeting in May of that year, the general court, in which there were twenty-four members of the corporation in addition to the governor, deputy governor and six assistants, proceded to enact important legislation. It was decided, however, that the court should thereafter be composed of deputies chosen by the freemen of every plantation. The body thus constituted should "have the full power & voyces of all the said ffreemen, deryved to them for the making & establishing of lawes, graunting of lands &c, . . . the matter of eleccion of magistrates & other officers onely excepted, wherein every freeman is to give his owne voyce." Thus a representative body was substituted for a primary body—a gathering of delegates, deputies, in the place of the full membership of the corporation.

This substitution was unquestionably made because the membership of the corporation was then large, consisting of over two hundred freemen. As Winthrop had suggested, such a body was too large for ordinary law-making even in that sturdy and competent colony; and moreover the inconveniences entailed, if that practice were followed, would be many. But it is explicit as any thing can be that the deputies carried with them the full power of the complete membership. It is difficult to assume—indeed I think quite impossible to assume—the change indicated a step forward in political liberty. That step was taken when the freemen, finding their rights under the corporate charter, asserted and obtained recognition of their power. The people of Massachusetts, those who were technically freemen, and presumably many others also, were undoubtedly not indifferent to the principles of political liberty; they were not neglectful of the principles which were at that time a matter of deep concern to the brethren they had left behind them in the mother country. But I am speaking of the substitution of a secondary (representative) body in the place of a primary body, and the insistence upon a legal right under the charter of a corporation; and this substitute can scarcely be looked up as a glorious and righteous system enshrined in English liberty. Probably even as early as 1634, the freemen had begun to think of themselves as citizens in a commonwealth; for the enlargement of the company membership and other influences probably marked for them, as it does for us, the silent transformation of the technically legal system of the corporation into something more; it marks the fact of the public character of the commonwealth. But the facts above related are to be remembered, if one wishes actually to know the conditions and the legal theory underlying and producing representation in Massachusetts. Representation was not gathered from the air; it was not some vague though luminous theory of right and liberty, but a convenient method of exercising fully legal right in a corporation.

The thing to be emphasized, however, is this: the representation *thus* set up made manifest a quality or characteristic of American representation; the very *origin* of the system in Massachusetts made clear that the deputies were *deputies*. They were clothed with the power belonging to the electorate. They carried with them the fact and the idea that the will of their constituents—the members of the corporation and the possessors of legal authority—was the source, under the charter, of governmental power. Now when you find that idea carried along until there is complete recognition in a democratic system of the principle that government is only the agent of the electorate and the political body, you are face to face with a salient idea of American constitutionalism. There is no danger of our over-stressing this basic idea, this elementary thought, that governmental power is exercised by direction and consent of the voter.[17]

17 It is of interest to notice that at a somewhat later time they made use of a proxy system, at least occasionally or optionally, in the election of officers. The first American case of the proxy was, I believe, in Maryland, and was a sort of stepping-stone between the primary body and the representative system. Maryland, it is true, was not a corporation, but a fief. And I may be quite wrong if I suggest corporate influences in that colony. One of the astonishing facts about the English colonies was the gradual but fairly speedy growth of institutional forms into substantial similarity. But the proxy system again emphasizes or makes plain the idea that the representative is deputized; he carries with him the power delegated to him.

If we would see with any clearness the influence of corporate forms, there are sundry other facts arresting our attention. Because of internal conditions and the necessities of the situation, the governor and assistants, even after representation was adopted, exercised considerable authority. The judicial system was largely, though not entirely, absorbed by the assistants or it developed naturally in that group. But more important is the change that came when the deputies and the assistants disagreed, and, indeed, for some years continued to disagree, concerning the power of the assistants in the meetings of the general court—now composed of the governor, deputy governor, assistants, and deputies. The assistants demanded recognition of what they called the "negative voice," i.e., the necessity of securing their consent to the determination of such questions as came before the meeting as a whole. The deputies declared decisions must be reached by a majority of the whole body. Though, by the terms of the corporate charter, a certain number of assistants must be of the quorum for the conduct of business, their right of veto is as least questionable.

This conflict, though based on differences of opinion and though caused by a difference of social outlook between the assistants and the deputies, was debated on the meaning of the charter of the corporation. The consequences of their disagreement was the establishment of the bicameral system. Again, this does not appear to be a purposeful copying of the English Parliamentary organization. The emergency arose in discussions concerning the conduct of the officers of a corporation; it is doubtful if the men of Massachusetts thought at all of the government across the sea. They may have done so; to me it seems very unlikely that such thought had any special influence. If you look therefore to the origins of the two-chambered legislature in the Massachusetts of the present day, you must go back to the old charter and the controversy between the "board of directors"—if I may use the modern term—and the representatives of the membership of the company. Near the end of the century, Massachusetts received a new charter; its institutional forms were similar to those which had grown up during the previous corporate history of the colony.

We have the right to assume that, in the case of the chartered colonies, particularly of the corporation colonies, the influence of a written document as the source of governmental authority, had effect on the development of American principles. Though the Massachusetts settlers were capable of developing their institutional forms and, with a cleverness not unknown to modern lawyers and statesmen, could find within the document, if need be, justification for doing as they desired, the elementary notion or underlying supposition, that the corporate authority was confined to the limits granted in a specific written instrument, in all probability not only conditioned the development of a constitution, but helped to create and perpetuate a principle or an attitude of mind. No corporation of the present or of the past has or had the legal power to go beyond the terms and boundaries of its charter.[18] I do not wish to overstress the similarity between constitutional limitations and the confines of a corporate charter; there are more evident and demonstrable sources of which we shall later speak and from which came the single salient characteristic of American constitutionalism, viz., the binding character of the written constitution. But certainly one cannot altogether neglect the probable effect— psychological effect, I may term it—of living for years under a government whose authority was confined, in theory, within written limitations.[19]

The influence of the Massachusetts system, as it developed out of the charter, in the first fifteen years, was very great. The scheme drawn up by the Connecticut settlers in their Fundamental Orders, was a distinct, and, presumably, a conscious imita-

[18] It is sometimes said that when a court declares a legislative act void, it does just what it does when it declares an act of a corporation ultra vires.

[19] I know it may well be said that the Massachusetts people, even in the decades preceding the annulment of the charter (1684), acted as if they were their own masters and could do as their inclination prompted. Their boldness and their independent spirit indeed speeded the dissolution of the company. But they did to some extent, at least, recognize the fact of charter limits.

tion of Massachusetts forms, as far as they had been developed.[20] The royal charter which was obtained by Connecticut in 1662, reproduced in essential particulars the institutional organization which the settlers had originally drawn up for themselves. The colony was thus definitely and legally established as a corporation on the place. Under that charter (whose workings were for a time disturbed by the Andros régime of a quarter of a century later) the colony continued to exist till the Revolution and beyond independence, till a new constitution was adopted in 1818.

It is not plain just how much the institutions of Plymouth were affected in their growth by the acts of the more powerful colony at the north. The leading settlers must have been acquainted with the organization of the Virginia Company under whose auspices they had expected to settle.[21] But in fact, the developments of Plymouth appear to have been largely, if not totally, the product of actual need and plain common sense. And yet here again appears the significant fact: whatever may have been the origin of their first organization, whatever may have been the effect of the old sea law or the church covenant, the Plymouth colony took on the outward form and the essential characteristics of a corporation.[22] The simple steps by which Plymouth formed its government in the early years is an entertaining example of the way in which the settlers adapted themselves to a situation and an example also of the influence, or the apparent influence, of the corporate structure.

It must be remembered that the settlement was

[20] Osgood in a careful summary presents the similarity of the institutions of the two colonies. **The American Colonies in the Seventeenth Century. I, The Chartered Colonies, Beginnings of Self-Government,** 309-311.

[21] Osgood, I, 291, surmises that the title and office of governor were borrowed from the Virginia Company. Here again we must remember that they chose a "governor" on board ship to act during the voyage, an officer suggested by the practice of the sea law to which we have referred.

[22] "Viewing the event from the standpoint of the colony, the meeting in the cabin of the Mayflower was in germ a general court, the signers of the compact were the earliest active citizens or freemen of Plymouth." Osgood, op. cit., I, 291. It must be remembered that the words "general court" signify the assembly of the members of a corporation.

more like a ranch, or a real plantation in the modern
sense of the word, than like anything else; and the
business system and forms of a corporation were by
no means inappropriate. The first officers—in addition to a captain, Miles Standish, for the direction
of military affairs—were a governor and an assistant.
The number of assistants was soon increased to five,
and then to seven. The main body of the freemen
constituted the general court. Before many years
passed, this body became a representative body for
legislative purposes, "committtees" being sent from
the towns to sit with the governor and assistants in
the general court. Individual members retained, however, the right to be present in person or by proxy
in the court of election and to participate in the
choosing of the governor and assistants. The bicameral system was not adopted. Thus in a very
simple way, as necessity indicated, the political
forms of the colony were shaped; they were in many
ways identical with the forms of Massachusetts Bay.
The basis was the corporate scheme of organization;
the results were, in essentials, the customary or orthodox form of colonial government. I mean by this,
that the *forms* were not essentially different from
the forms of the other corporate colonies; nor did
they differ so very much even from those of the
royal and proprietary colonies.

The written ballot—not, it is true, a part of the
constitutional system as such—was early used in
the colonies. What was its origin, the probable or
possible source of the idea, in addition to plain common sense? The ballot, presumably in written form,
was used by the Virginia Company. A large portion
of that company were, it appears, Puritans. "They
introduced the democratic ballot-box in place of
viva-voce voting."[23] In Massachusetts the ballot was

[23] A. E. McKinley, **The Suffrage Franchise in the Thirteen English
Colonies in America,** 18, 310, 311. "At the outset the Massachusetts
Company did not adopt the ballot in its elections, as we have seen
that the London Company did many years earlier, but held its
elections in London by 'erection of hands.' As early as 1629, the
ballot was used in the church at Salem, and shortly after the trans-
mission of the charter to New England it was adopted in the Company's elections. It was originally used in the election of governor,
the first occasion probably being the election of May, 1634; and in
September 1635, was extended to the elections of deputies to the
general court."

used in 1634, for the election of governor; the next year it was extended to the election of deputies. It was also early used in some of the town elections. The fundamental Orders of Connecticut provided that the electors should "bring the names of such, written in severall papers, as they desire to have chosen." Proof is lacking; but the whole process and its adoption indicate the influence of the corporation, though, with the exception of the Virginia Company, the prevailing practice in the large trading-companies appears to have been the raising of hands. Not till after the Reform Bill of 1867 was the written ballot used for the choice of members of the House of Commons in Britain.

In the early days when institutions were taking shape, the political forms and customs of England probably had effect; certainly they had considerable effect at a later time. But it will hardly do, as we have shown, for example, in the case of the bicameral system in Massachusetts, to leave the corporation and its institutional forms out of consideration. A learned writer says: "Our State and Federal system of two chambers and veto-possessing governor or president, are remnants of the old theory of mixed government." As a matter of fact, bicameralism in America did not originate in any theory, as far as I can discover. If we turn to the ordinance passed by the Virginia Company in 1621, we find, it is true, the government in Virginia was required to imitate the policy and the form of government "used in the realm of England"; but the provision assigning the veto to the governor cannot be considered a distinct imitation of the royal veto, but rather as a continuation of the governor's power for the protection of the interests of the corporation. At least, this is certain: the first provision for the veto appears in orders of a trading-company and cannot be looked upon as the result of a design to imitate the purely English system of government.

One other matter, and we have finished, for the time being, consideration of the corporation as a source of American doctrines, or, to speak less assuredly, as an undoubted source of some American institutions, and as the *probable* source of certain distinct institutional principles. Charles Francis Adams sought to establish the "charter origin of the New England town." It is impossible, I believe, to banish, as that distinguished authority did, the English parish and the English town, from any large view of the forces begetting the New England town, the one institution which has received from students of politics more comprehensive praise than any other form of political order and government in the American system. Mr. Adams himself said: "The town-meeting has, in fact, been the one feature in American polity which no one has as yet seen fit to criticise adversely." The article in which Mr. Adams announced his theory was a vigorous attack upon the so-called Germanic origin of the New England towns —that theory of inheritance, or survival, or reversion, characteristic of a biological interpretation of history, which held much vogue and was so widely accepted from thirty to fifty years ago. He contended that the town was essentially indigenous, not a copy of English local system or an inheritance from remote and shadowy ancestors.

This at least we may be confident about: the New England town was a business enterprise, connected of course in some measure with religion; the town-meeting does bear a resemblance to the general court of the corporation; the proprietors, to whom the land was granted by the general court, constituted, in miniature, a land company, not dissimilar in its outward seeming to the larger formally constituted corporations. But all of these similarities do not necessarily prove the charter—or the corporation—origin of the town. Let us be content with saying that in any study of the genesis and the structure of that much-lauded system of local government, a system, which with some modifications has extended westward across the continent, the influence of the corporate forms and practices must be taken into

consideration.[24] At all events the business character
of the undertaking cannot be ignored.

As I have already suggested, the circumstances
under which representation was established appear
to be of importance for an understanding of the
Revolutionary argument against Britain. American
representation has been characterized from the beginning by this feature: the person chosen as a
representative is a resident and a member of the community—the town, the county, the district, or other
local body—which elects him; and he is supposed to
voice the will of the people of that community; he,
as one of themselves, carries the voice of the voters
to legislative halls. Whether this fact necessitates,
by any inevitable implication, that the representative, when once chosen, should rigorously obey what
may appear to be the desire of his district, and that
he is by political ethic bound to surrender his own
opinion if it be different from that of his constituents,
is a question which we need not discuss. Possibly it
is enough to say there is a formal method of expressing authoritative opinion concerning governmental policy; and in a given area the method is by
formal election of the representative, not by resolutions of mass-meetings after an election. The fact
that the person chosen is at the time of his election a
member of the community and continues to be a
member gives very substantial, if not complete, as-

[24] "Thus the Massachusetts town-meeting was in its origin the
meeting of the body of proprietors of the corporation for the trans-
action of corporate affairs. Such was the beginning of the system,
—in its character commercial and modern, and not feudal or primitive; legal, and not ecclesiastical." Charles Francis Adams, **The
Genesis of the Massachusetts Town,** in Massachusetts Historical Society **Proceedings,** (Jan. 1892), 205. "The colony was in its charter
termed a 'plantation'; and now the towns were subordinate planta-
tions, and so called. Those who settled in the localities created into
towns or townships were the planters, the proprietors, and the inhabitants. In other words, they were the beneficiaries or stockholders
in an incorporated business enterprise; and they acted always in
strict accordance with this legal position." Ibid., 201. In the discussion before the Society, Edward Channing defended the parish origin
with force and learning. Osgood's discussion is of course significant:
"Experiences, suggestions, customary modes of action derived from
the manor, the village, the hamlet, the parish, probably influenced
the course of action of the first settlers, though no written evidence
of the process appears. The town was an adaptation of well-known
English forms of local settlement to new, or at least modified, conditions of the beginning." **The American Colonies in the Seventeenth
Century,** I, 426.

surance of his representing the opinion of the community.

Now the absence of that practice in Britain, the fact that the men of one borough may choose and frequently do choose, as their member in the House of Commons, someone resident in a distant region, certainly obscures the fundamental notion of representation, as America conceived and conceives representation. It may be said, with little exaggeration, the representative practices of Britain at the time of the American Revolution were scarcely more than a method which was used for filling the benches of the House. The system did not involve the principle that the member was elected to carry with him the voice and the will of his constituents. He represented them and the rest of the people of the Empire, and he did so in the sense of having the power and the duty of protecting the interests of the whole people, not merely voicing the desires of his constituents or obeying their commands. It is easy to see, therefore, how the Britons in Parliament one hundred and sixty years ago and more could in effect say to the Americans, "We represent you; we are charged with the duty of caring for your welfare."

The essential American idea that the representative is the agent of the electors is partly due to the way in which representation originated. I have intimated, even if I have not demonstrated, the connection between the corporation, as a quasi-body-politic, and the beginnings of representation, by deputies and proxies. In the case of Massachusetts, whose practices strongly affected the rest of New England, representation began during the early processes of adaptation of a corporate charter to the needs of a commonwealth. In a corporation, authority, the authority which is the source of administrative power and action, rests in the main body of its membership. The source of authority was the freemen, and the deputy was the vehicle by and through which the will of the freemen was expressed. Thus we see the basis, the fundamental groundwork, of the democratic idea, that people are the possessors of power and government is their agent. This historical evidence might be enlarged upon; we might, for example, point to the town-meeting and its elections of selectmen and sundry other officials; we might refer again to the forms and practices of the Puritan churches. If objection be made to any such generalization, because the beginnings in Virginia were different from those of Massachusetts, it may still be well to notice that even in Virginia representation was set up by a corporation, and the underlying thought seems to have been that the people should thus have a voice in the management of their own affairs; even in this early primitive assembly there appeared more or less vaguely the idea or the principle which I have attempted briefly to describe—the principle and the underlying idea that the source of authority is the people. The subject is too large for complete examination. This, however, is obvious: in one way and another the colonists had brought into fairly clear relief, particularly in the choice of their representatives in the popular assembly, a principle—though possibly many of them were for a long time not quite conscious of it—that government received from them its power to act. And of course this idea, if made actual, is the basis of democracy and popular government. It is not representation as an institutional process, but the principle of political power on which true representation rests, which is the important thing.

When one is dealing with imponderables, it is well not to be positive. It is impossible to demonstrate by documentary evidence that the essential qualities of American representation are due to the way in which it began; but in any attempt at understanding, one is inevitably led back to the very beginnings; and he finds those beginnings produced and shaped by actual American conditions; he discovers little or no evidence of a copying of English institutions as such.[25]

[25] I have no desire to deny the influence of British institutions and especially of British constitutional principles which were thought to be, as they were on the whole, admirable protection for personal rights. That fact I have already dwelt upon. In the history of the colonies, more noticeably I think in the colonies south and west of New England, countless references were made by the colonies, especially in the eighteenth century, to the political system of Britain. My contention is only this, that the representative system was not set up in the earliest colonies in imitation of the English House of Com-

It may be well also to remember that there were inequalities in the system of colonial representation; not only was suffrage limited, but representative areas differed one from the other in population; the western portion of a colony was discriminated against, and the older section were favored; there was respect for established social position and wealth, and at least in later days there was in the minds of some leaders the idea that property as such had the right to be represented. The American conception of representation is, however, to be understood by a study of the actual origin of the system.

We may now consider the way in which this fundamental notion of representation came into conflict with the British practices and theories, in the decade of argument before the Revolutionary War. The English idea of representation in the eighteenth century was described and defended by George Grenville of Stamp Act fame. He referred to the fact that large numbers of British people had no vote. "The Colonies," he said, "are in exactly the same Situation: All British Subjects are really in the same; none are actually, all are virtually represented in Parliament; for every Member of Parliament sits in the House, not a Representative of his own Constituents, but as one of that august Assembly by which all the Commons of Great Britain are represented. Their Rights and their Interests, however his own Borough may be affected by general Dispositions, ought to be the great Objects of his Attention,

mons, nor was there, so far as I have been able to discover, any exaltation of the representative system; it was adopted because it was a convenient method of meeting the needs of a situation, and was not so much an acquisition of new popular power as a suitable method of exercising it. This can hardly be gainsaid in the case of the New England colonies established before 1650; and it is true of the origin of representation in Maryland, which, it is true, began as a fief and not as a corporation. If we are to speak in the terms of unsentimental historical fact, we are obliged to speak with some doubt and hesitation of England's gift of representation to America, when we have in mind its beginning in the first half of the seventeenth century.

If this still seems altogether inconclusive, the reader may at least think of Plymouth. Can it be supposed that the people of Plymouth thought of themselves as taking a step forward in political liberty when they decided, because of the inconveniences caused by winter snows and summer sand, to forgo the meeting of all and to let delegates act for them, while they retained as a body the privilege of choosing the main administrative officers?

and the only Rules for his Conduct; and to sacrifice these to a partial Advantage in favour of the Place where he was chosen, would be a Departure from his Duty; if it were otherwise, Old Sarum would enjoy Privileges essential to Liberty, which are denied to Birmingham and to Manchester; but as it is, they and the Colonies and all British Subjects whatever, have an equal Share in the general Representation of the Commons of *Great Britain,* and are bound by the Consent of the Majority of that House, whether their own particular Representatives consented to or opposed the Measures there taken, or whether they had or had not particular Representatives there."[26]

As a favorable and complimentary description of the British system, this statement cannot be improved upon. Grenville certainly scores when he insists upon the impropriety of subjecting the general interests of the Empire to the particular needs of a locality; and we cannot well question the disadvantage of our own system, which often presents the picture of local representatives struggling valiantly for their particular districts and exhibiting no mastering desire to evaluate the needs of our empire as a whole. But how absurd it must have seemed to a man of Massachusetts, this notion of his being represented in that "august Assembly" by the member for Old Sarum; for in Old Sarum there lived not a single person; by processes which may easily be described, ploughed fields, not people, were represented.[27] And if Old Sarum is the traditional example of British representation, while populous places like Birmingham and Manchester sent to the Commons no members at all, it was in fact only slightly more conspicuous than some other borough. "Burgages under water-courses," says Mr. Porritt, "ploughed fields like those at Old Sarum; deeds which could not convey any property which could be seized either for taxes or for debts, like those at Droitwich;

---

[26] G. Grenville, **Regulations,** etc., 109.

[27] "This spot," wrote Samuel Curwen, an American who was in England from 1775 to 1783, "which in former days was the site of Old Sarum, containing about sixty acres, unless I am misinformed, without one house on it, is now entitled to send two members to Parliament." E. Porritt, **The Unreformed House of Commons,** I,36.

coal-houses, pigeon-lofts and pig-styes, on which burgage franchises were based at Richmond; and plots of land at Ludgershall so small that they might be covered with a hearth-stone, continued to confer the right to vote for members of the House of Commons."[28] It is an amusing and entertaining fact that, after the awakening of the political consciousness begotten by the American and French Revolutions, there were instances in which men bought their seats from a borough-monger, that they might combat the injustice and the vices of the whole system. All of this, of course, shows not only the basis for fundamental antagonism and misunderstanding between America and Britain a hundred and sixty years ago, but the fact of America's standing for essential and elementary principles of free popular government.

And in fact a step forward had been taken when a man who had bought his seat in Parliament felt himself under no obligation to obey the dictates of the great landholder who held title to the ploughed fields or pig-sties which had the privilege of selecting a member of the Commons.

Why did the Americans of Revolutionary days not point fingers of scorn at British so-called representation? Otis, on one occasion exclaimed, "To what purpose is it to ring the everlasting changes to the colonists on the cases of Manchester, Birmingham and Sheffield, who return no members? If those now so considerable places are not represented, they ought to be."[29] But the Americans did not commonly suggest the need of revising the British system and adapting it to reality and to principles. Indeed, one of the underlying difficulties in the way of settling the dispute with the colonies was that an acceptance of the American argument by the British Parliamentarian would logically demolish the very basis of the British House, and would discredit, and more than discredit, the equitable right of members of Parliament to hold their own places. And if we add to this the influence of graft, the spoils system which

[28] Ibid., 38.
[29] Considerations on Behalf of the Colonists in a Letter to a Noble Lord, (London, 1765), 6.

the British had developed to a high degree of efficiency, and the control which the aristocracy held over both chambers of the British Parliament, we see how great was the difficulty of reconciliation between the mother country and her self-assertive children across the sea.

The question asked above requires further examination. The failure of the Americans to criticize and condemn the whole British system is in fact of considerable significance, because it makes clear a characteristic of the Revolution to which attention will be paid in a later lecture. We cannot say that the Revolutionary leaders were entirely unaware of the absurdities of this system. They instinctively thought of representation more or less abstractly; but the abstraction was given a degree of concreteness by their own experience. But there was more than this. As a practical matter, an attack on the British system, which might imply the necessity of a complete abandonment of the ridiculous method of filling the Commons' benches, would probably awaken bitter opposition. Such opposition was to be avoided especially in the earlier days when the outspoken desire of even the radical leaders was for continued loyalty and certainly for the maintenance and preservation of their own institutions.

The most fundamental thing, however, appears to be this. The Americans did not pose as revolutionists. They were satisfied[30] with what they had; at all events, such was the main content of their argument; they had their own institutions, they were not engaged in a crusade to improve the institutions of Britain; they resisted intrusion and pictured the Parliamentarians as innovators; they based their claim on English history and took seriously—and not, I think, with their tongues in their cheeks—the glorified phrases commonly attached to English representation. They found support in their opposition to Parliamentary taxation by declaring that the princi-

[30] Some one may say the back-country people were not satisfied because they were subject to discrimination. But the position of the colonies was this: they were not setting out to "new model" the English representative system, but to insist upon the rights of their own elected representatives.

ple of no taxation without representation was embodied in the British constitution.

This failure to ridicule Old Sarum and Droitwich and to resent the folly of allowing pig-sties to elect men to Parliament and this absence of condemnation for the prevalent practice of purchasing seats in the House are significant. The Americans claimed their share in the British constitution; and unless they assumed that British representation actually existed, their cause, as they conceived it, would be damaged and their main argument would be inapplicable. Just how much they were consciously impressed by the logical necessity of refraining from criticism of Britain's institutions, I cannot say; but nevertheless, nothing else appears so clearly to demonstrate the conservative temper of the Revolution.

George Grenville's argument, as quoted above, purports to be a defense of virtual representation, as distinguished from what he considered actual representation. Now there is something to be said for the theory of virtual representation. Daniel Dulany was willing to acknowledge the justice of the doctrine under certain conditions: "The Electors who are inseparably connected in their Interests with the Non-Electors may be justly deemed to be the Representatives of the Non-Electors." To state the case differently, if a member of the Commons and those upon whom the burden of taxation falls have the same interest, each bearing his share of the burden, the doctrine of virtual representation is not utterly unsound, even if it be not wholly in accord with the spirit of full-fledged democracy. But such was not the case when the Parliamentarian saw fit to tax the colonies, in order that the load carried by himself and his constituents might be lightened. The absurdity of the doctrine when applied to the Empire could not fail to make its appeal to the average colonist; the attempt to justify the British system and apply it to the dominions across the seas was a tragic blunder.

The shrewdest defenders of Parliamentary power sought to answer the American argument as far as it rested on the basis of compact. The colonists, if we may take Sam Adams as their spokesman, insisted that, in accord with the principle of natural right, no government could take property from any one without his consent. At the same time they argued that the British government was founded on compact and thus rested on the consent of the governed. So, said the British pamphleteer, money is not taken from you without your consent, because it is taken by the government to which you have consented. The social-compact theory, in its baldest form, does not necessarily imply continuous representation and repeated consent to every act of government resulting from the compact. It is true that Locke took for granted an elected legislature; but the development of the principle of representation marks a somewhat advanced stage of the compact-theory.

We are here interested, however, not in the blunders of British statesmanship. The cardinal fact is America's conception of representation of people, as the basis of really popular government; or—shall we say?—we are interested in the long effort, not as yet entirely successful, to build up and make actual the principle that power belongs to the people at large. This idea, call it political democracy if you will, was not fully realized in the Revolutionary epoch; many men of probity and honor feared the populace; suffrage was commonly restricted. But this one essential idea gained sufficient impetus to be carried out, in form at least, before many decades and must be listed among the principles of American Constitutionalism.

III

The Social Compact and its Significance in America

IN THE FIRST lecture, attention was called to the words of Robert Browne asserting that the general principles which he had announced were applicable to the civil state. It is my purpose now to discuss briefly the principles of the social-compact philosophy, which has played a very important rôle in English and American constitutional history. And it is largely because of the importance of this philosophy that I have given so much time to the discussion of the two types of association considered in the preceding lectures. If Browne's assertions were unique, or if the formation of churches by covenant was of significance only in the history of church polity, we should not need to pay much attention to the practice or the theory. In discussing this theory of compact and its prevalence, I shall be laying the basis for understanding the American Revolutionary arguments, and for understanding also the fundamental principles in the character of American constitutions.

The theory or principle of the origin of society and government in compact, which I have sought to connect with the foundation of the Separatist church and also, though with less assurance, with the foundations and the essential character of the trading company, played a great rôle in history. Our appreciation of it is especially necessary for the interpretation of American constitutional history. We should badly distort the facts, however, if we should assume that the origin of the theory is to be found only within the two fields of interest and endeavor of which I have spoken. These two fields, the church and the business corporation, have been emphasized in the preceding pages because of their special influence in America and particularly in New England. But one cannot seek the source of any widely held and widely used theory and be confident of the exact time and place of birth. The fact is, this compact-theory was, in some of its aspects, so old, it had so many manifestations, or was so often propounded at least as pure theory, that confidence concerning origin and descent is quite undesirable. My emphasis is, however, laid upon the actual and concrete utilization of the theory of compact in English history and even more in American history of the seventeenth and eighteenth centuries. I wish in this lecture to make the reality of this doctrine perfectly plain.

The Declaration of Independence contains a peculiarly clear and systematic, though brief, announcement of the origin of government in compact, the natural equality of men, and other implications of contractual relationship. But the Declaration was not new: Jefferson and the Continental Congress would have been guilty of folly had they attempted at that juncture to stage a revolution on purely novel theories, unknown and unrecognized by the common man. The main doctrines of the Declaration were familiar, especially so to the New Englanders; in some respects they were of hoary antiquity. Dr. Sullivan, seeking beginnings finds them long before the Christian era—the New England theologians would scarcely stop short of the Garden of Eden—and says, "Thus, by Cicero's time (106-43 B.C.) there were three ideas of the Declaration known to the world." (He must mean, I think, had been announced by philosophers.) "These were, first, the conscious instituting of government by men, held by Protagoras, the Sophists, and the Epicureans; second, the equality of men—an idea advanced by the Stoics; and third, the idea of natural rights developed by Cicero. . . . It remained for one of the writers during the Conciliar Movement in the early part of the fifteenth century—Nicholas of Cusa

—to take all the doctrines of the Declaration and combine them into a systematic whole. 'Since all men,' he says, 'are by nature free, then government rests on the consent of the governed.' "[1]

In the middle of the seventeenth century John Milton laid down this positive declaration: "No man, who knows aught, can be so stupid to deny, that all men naturally were born free, being the image and resemblance of God himself, and were, by privilege above all the creatures, born to command, and not to obey: and that they live so, till from the root of Adam's transgression, falling among themselves to do wrong and violence, and foreseeing that such courses must needs tend to the destruction of them all, they agreed by common league to bind each other from mutual injury, and jointly to defend themselves against any that gave disturbance and opposition to such agreement. Hence came cities, towns, and commonwealths."[2] You may answer to this assertion, that all of us are so stupid as to deny Milton's pronouncements *in toto,* so stupid as to ridicule the establishment of human society and government in any formal original compact, and so perverse, some of us, as to disbelieve that human violence is the fruit of Adam's transgression. But our disbelief need not lead us to neglect, or throw aside as trivial, doctrines and theories which were of tremendous influence in the two centuries and more after Browne wrote his pamphlet and after the Separatists set up their little assemblies and suffered persecution. Milton's doctrines of the mid-seventeenth century underlay the principles of the American Revolution of the eighteenth.

Such theories as those just mentioned were not confined to the England of Milton's time. Thomas Hooker, the founder of Connecticut, declared: "Among such who by no impression of nature, no rule of providence, or appointment from God or

[1] James Sullivan, **The Antecedents of the Declaration of Independence,** The American Historical Association, **Annual Report,** (1902), I, 67-81.

[2] Milton, **Tenure of Kings and Magistrates. Prose Works,** (Griswold ed.) I, 377.

reason have power each over other; there must of
necessity be a mutual engagement each of the other,
by their free con(s)ent, before by any rule of God
they have any right or power, or can exercise either,
each towards the other. This appears in all covenants betwixt Prince and People, Husband and Wife,
Master and Servant, and most palpable is the expression of this in all confederations and corporations . . . they should *first freely ingage* themselves
in such covenants, and then be careful to fulfil such
duties." John Cotton, teacher of the Boston church,
pronounced the same theories; they were the common possession of the men of New England, as they
were the common possession of the more advanced
Puritan leaders of the rebellion against the Stuarts.
"It is evident," said Cotton, "by the light of nature,
that all civill Relations are founded in Covenant. For
to pass by natural Relations between Conquerors
and Captives; there is no other way whereby a people *sui Juris* free from naturall and compulsory en-
gagements, can be united or combined together into
one visible body to stand by mutuall Relations, fel-
low-members of the same body but only by mutual
Covenant; as appeareth between husband and wife
in the family, Magistrates and subjects in the Commonwealth, fellow-citizens in the same cities."[3]

These quotations are but examples of the fact I
have wished to set forth; they not only illustrate but
they demonstrate the currency of certain cardinal
principles in old and New England during the seventeenth century. We also find in these quotations evidence of a fact, which we often lose sight of, that
there was a more or less intimate connection between the men of old England and the men who
had crossed the ocean. Those who remained at
home, that great body of Independents who before
the middle of the seventeenth century took up the
struggle against Charles I, watched with anxious
attention the progress of the new England across
the sea; and from this side of the water the settlers,

[3] Some of the above quotations are to be found in Charles Borgeaud, **The Rise of Modern Democracy in Old and New England,**
which treats in an illuminating way the connection between religious
and political thinking, 84n, 85-86, etc.

forming their churches and developing their political system, were intensely interested in the controversies of the land they had left behind them. It is noteworthy that both John Cotton's, *The Way of the Churches of Christ in New England,* and Thomas Hooker's, *A Survey of the Summe of Church Discipline*—the two books from which excerpts were given a moment ago—were published in England, as were sundry other pamphlets from their pens. In a sermon preached in New England in 1640, this sense of kindred purpose is plainly put forth. "How have they alwayes listened after our welfare. . . . How doe they (I meane the multitudes of well-affected persons there) talk of *New-England* with delight! . . . And when sometimes a *New-England* man returnes thither, how is he lookt upon, . . . entertained, the ground hee walks upon beloved for his sake, and the house held the better where hee is? how are his words listened to, laid up, and related frequently when hee is gone? neither is any love or kindnesse held too much for such a man."[4]

It is necessary now to do something in the way of demonstrating the truth of my assertions concerning the prevalence of the idea of compact, especially among the New Englanders, whose thinking in politics and religion, in church polity and theology, was so distinctly the thinking of seventeenth-century Puritanism. The philosophy underlying the Puritan revolt against Charles I and the philosophy of the American Revolution were similar; we may indeed say essentially identical in character. But this similarity is not enough to satisfy us. An unbroken line of descent can be traced. And the tracing of this line is advisable if we wish to see our indebtedness to the past and how firmly fixed were certain fundamental notions concerning the organization of a state and the establishment of its institutions.

If we trace this line even incompletely and see the

4 William Hooke, **New Englands Teares for Old Englands Feares,** reprinted in facsimile in S. H. Emery, **The Ministry of Taunton,** Boston, 1853, I, 96. Cf. George P. Gooch, **The History of English Democratic Ideas in the Seventeenth Century,** 93. Original in the Thomason Collection.

continuity of these doctrines, we do not need to suppose that the men of the American Revolution only rummaged about during an anxious emergency to find in Milton, Sidney, or Locke a support for the position they were prepared to take against George III. Those writers of seventeenth-century England were known and used by the Americans in their protests against king and Parliament; but the point is that the New Englanders in their own history had kept these principles in their primitive and compelling simplicity. We must remember the New England clergymen's position. They were leaders in their community; they continued to be the leaders till the development of commercial activity and especially the Revolutionary ferment gave new opportunity for lawyers to exercise their wits and exhibit their learning; and indeed I know no better term than "lawyer" to describe the intellectual outlook of the minister, who saw the world as a world of law and pictured the divine judge upon the throne distributing justice and administering the mandates of an unchangeable jurisprudence in accord with His covenants and in conformity with natural law and reason.

During the Revolution and in the process of setting up new governments, the preachers played a conspicuous rôle. The philosophy of the seventeenth century was repeated over and over again by New England divines, who preached about a law of reason and a law of God, the sacredness of covenant and the divine character of government. A wilful government, disregarding the good of the people, was in conflict with the law of the ruler of the universe. But these doctrines were not new to the Puritan minister. They can be seen in the election sermons of the later seventeenth century and the first half of the eighteenth century; they are to be found in occasional controversial pamphlets, as well as in the sermons and other declarations of the Revolutionary period.

I have been stressing the idea of association, the process of merger, the way in which a body with authority and governmental power could be formed.

But it is necessary to notice also that this conception of a contractual relationship permeated the theology of advanced Puritanism. It is, I imagine, always difficult for men to carry out, or to entertain side by side, two differing or contradictory ideas. We are not likely to habituate ourselves to distinctly conflicting methods of thought or methods of approach to an intellectual problem. More certainly will this difficulty exist if men are definitely rationalistic in their thinking. If they subject the organization or the policy of the church to rational analysis and reject everything that will not stand the attack of reason, they are not likely to be content with accepting theology based on a different philosophy. However that may be, the salient fact is that in the theology of the New England Puritan, derived from an exhaustive study of the scriptures, the conception of a covenant or contractual relationship was prominent; probably we should be justified in saying dominant and central. *"It has pleased God all along from the beginning of the World to transact with man in a Covenant way ... God never has made but two Covenants with man:* which are ordinarily distinguish'd into, the *Covenant of Works,* and the *Covenant of Grace."*[5]

Though I may weary you by repetitions, I venture once again to call your attention to the essential qualities of the compact-or covenant-thinking: first, the individual existed and he had right of self-determination; second, he with others could form a body—a church or a state—which would have real existence and, within its scope, real power. We may now turn to the philosopher of the seventeenth century, who in the field of politics put forth these doctrines with special cogency and clearness. John Locke's *Two Treatises of Government* was published just after the English Revolution of 1688, and was intended in part to defend the principles of that revolution. These essays and especially his famous second essay were very influential for a century and

[5] Williams, William, **An Essay to Prove the Interest of the Children of Believers in the Covenant,** Boston (1727), 5-6. Quoted by Charles Francis Adams, **Three Episodes of Massachusetts History,** I, 402, 403.

more after they were written. Locke declared, as had others before him, that there was a state of nature. In that state of nature men have perfect freedom, within the bounds of the law of nature, and complete equality. But as each man is a judge in his own case, the execution of the law of nature being in his own hands, there is need of government. No man, however, "can be put out of this estate and subjected to the political power of another without his own consent, which is done by agreeing with other men, to join and unite into a community for their comfortable, safe, and peaceable living, one amongst another, in a secure enjoyment of their properties, and a greater security against any that are not of it." This is that "consent of the governed," which Jefferson announced in the Declaration of Independence.[6]

In New England, twenty years before Locke wrote, John Davenport outlined the organization of civil society in compact, as indeed he had done some years before in his *Power of the Congregational Churches;* and the same doctrines were variously and often repeated in later years.[7] We can find the compact-system more explicitly presented early in the eighteenth century by a Massachusetts divine. John Wise made the whole relationship and the whole process of contract perfectly clear:

"Let us conceive in our mind a multitude of men, all naturally free and equal; going about voluntarily, to erect themselves into a new common-wealth.

"I. They must interchangeably each man covenant to join in one lasting society, that they may be cap-

[6] It may be well to point out again that theories of this kind were not original by any means with Locke or with the Puritans. Thomas Aquinas declared that a thing is made in two ways, by the law of nature and by a certain compact made among men. See W. G. de Burgh, **The Legacy of the Ancient World**, 387; "Modern constitutionalism is the child of the Middle Age," ibid., 395.

[7] The continuance of this thinking and the part of the preachers in maintaining it is brought out clearly and convincingly in Miss Alice M. Baldwin's **The New England Clergy and the American Revolution.** To the student of American constitutional doctrine Miss Baldwin's chapter on "The Legalism of Theology and Church Polity" is especially valuable. She makes no pretense of showing the intimate association between the legalism and American constitutionalism, but the associations can with no reasonableness be doubted. See also Davenport's defense of covenants and compacts, ibid., 25, 26.

able to concert the measures of their safety, by a public vote.

"2. A vote or decree must then nextly pass to set up some particular species of government over them. And if they are joined in their first compact upon absolute terms to stand to the decision of the first vote concerning the species of government: then all are bound by the majority to acquiesce in that particular form thereby settled, though their own private opinion, incline them to some other model.

"3. After a decree has specified the particular form of government, then there will be need of a new covenant, whereby those on whom sovereignty is conferred, engage to take care of the common peace, and welfare. And the subjects on the other hand, to yield their faithful obedience. In which covenant is included that submission and union of wills, by which a state may be conceived to be but one person. . . . A civil state is a compound moral person."[8]

This is a very thorough and logical presentation of the contract-idea; it contains by implication the distinction between the state and the government, which is characteristic of the American system. The definition of the state, moreover, will not appear altogether weird and fanciful to the modern political philosopher, even though he cast aside as ridiculous the successive contracts. It is noticeable, too, that the contracts—one holding the people in the union of all, the other binding the government to the people—are similar to the early covenants of the church, of which we have spoken.

The continuity of this theory of religious and civil organization is perfectly plain; and furthermore, lest one may think these pronouncements had no effect on the Revolutionary period and had no interest for the men of that late day, we may notice John Wise's treatises, *The Churches Quarrel Espoused*, which was published in 1710, and his *A Vindication of the Government of New England Churches* already

[8] **Vindication of the Government of New England**, (1772 ed.), 17-39. Quoted by Miss Baldwin, ibid., 28, 29.

quoted, which was published in 1717. Early in 1772 an edition of these two tracts was published in Boston, "and so eager was the perusal of them, and so extensive the demand for their clear reasoning in favor of democracy as the **best** government, that another edition, of which more than one thousand copies were bespoken before its issue, was put to press in the same city in the same year.[9] That is an evidence of popularity of which any modern publicist might well be envious. John Wise's pamphlets must be placed on the list of best sellers in the critical days of the Revolutionary discussion.

We thus see how prevalent and how dominating was this theory of compact. Even God was not all powerful; He was bound, bound by His own promises and His own contracts, limited by the nature of His own being; He was not capable of breaking His own law. He was a sovereign, a king of kings and princes, but His government was not absolute or arbitrary government. In other words, as men were prepared to deny unlimited authority of the earthly monarch and his unqualified powers as the head of the state; and as they were intent upon discovering in written documents the form of church order, and the nature of church worship; and as they established their own churches by free association, so also they saw by light of their own reasoning the whole celestial and terrestrial universe to be a universe of law, by which the sovereign was bound, and by which He had bound himself.[10]

As students of constitutional history we are not interested in either church polity or theology for themselves; but we are necessarily interested in an all-pervading idea. I have spoken of the learning and amazing skill with which the clergymen developed their doctrines. Most of us have not the inclination,

[9] H. M. Dexter, **Congregationalism as Seen in Its Literature,** 501.

[10] It has been said that political liberty is the product of religious animosities. But an aphorism of that kind though brilliant is likely to contain or suggest too much. I do not think anyone would seriously contend that zeal for ecclesiastical independence or liberty was the sole source of political liberty. We cannot, however, deny, as the pages above clearly indicate, I think, that these animosities, religious cravings, and ambitions, had great effect.

the training, or the intellectual devotion necessary for understanding them; we find it difficult or impossible to thread the mazes of the whole intricate and complex theological system. But this, I venture to say, is plain: the atmosphere in which the theologian worked was that of the court-room; his methods of approach and reasoning were essentially legalistic; he started with a written document; he applied his logical faculties to its interpretation and to the application of its teachings and its examples or precedents. To me, though as a layman I must modestly acknowledge the limitations of ignorance, the whole bears a distinct resemblance to constitutional law. Churches were formed in direct accord with scriptural teaching; ministers and, indeed, civil officials were held to be the vicegerents of God. Though church officers could be freely chosen, they were subjects of the Most High. The essential unity (or the essential harmony) in theological and political doctrine, is perfectly evident.[11]

The legalistic or extreme rationalistic character of Puritanism is humorously presented in Oliver Wendell Holmes' *The Deacon's Masterpiece; or The Wonderful One-Hoss Shay*. And we should not go far wrong if we selected the poet's pronouncement as the guiding watchword of the Puritan preacher: "Logic is logic. That's all I say." Such certainly it appeared to be to the genial humorist in his quaint satire. As the world and the starry heavens were to be understood by the application of reason; so even the one-hoss shay, "that was built in such a logical way it ran a hundred years to a day," was the creature and the product of pure logic. And there was something more than this: the preacher exalted reason, of which God was the embodiment or—

[11] I have not sought to present any study of the doctrine of Calvinism or the extent of Calvin's influence on English or American protestantism. It may be that I have over-emphasized influence of Separatism as such; but I do not think so. If anyone wishes to insist upon the dominating influence of the Genevan reformer, the main lines of Puritanic doctrines, whatever the source of the ideas, are the matters of consequence. "**Calvin's Institutes of the Christian Religion** was the chief religious and political text-book of the English Puritans." Osgood, **The American Colonies in the Seventeenth Century,** I, 201.

more properly speaking, perhaps—of which He was the great expositor; reason was the unchanging and unchangeable law of the universe. They, of course, repudiated mysticism or any process of reaching truth save by intellectual attention to the law as laid down in the scriptures. One needs only to examine the history and the fate of Anne Hutchinson, the heroine of the Antinomian controversy of 1636-7, to see how intensely the Puritan leaders of Massachusetts detested mysticism or the awful idea that God spake in His own voice to the searching soul in the primitive colony as He spake to Moses and the prophets of old.[12] Anne ventured to deny the leadership of the learned of the church and the state; she dared to go beyond the realm of their logic and to preach a covenant of grace as the assured foundation of everlasting salvation. The dominance of rationalism was not confined to the early seventeenth century; if it were, I should not be speaking about it at length. It, of course, persisted; and the whole régime of which I have been speaking must be borne in mind in any attempt to understand the theories of the Revolution and the formation of American constitutions.

All this rationalism, all this conception of a universe governed by law and reason, is of immense consequence in the religious and constitutional history of New England. If men had originally established the state by agreement or consent one with another (as the Separatists established this church by covenanting with God and their fellow-believers), the same thing might be done again. Men could form constitutional compacts, and by them, if they so desired, explicitly prescribe the limits of governmental power. Men would never have left a state of freedom in order to put themselves under the bondage of an

12 There is no doubt a strange inconsistency between this excited denial that God spoke directly to Anne and the fact that the men of those times saw the hand of God and His teachings in trivial matters. But the contradiction is easily explained by the circumstances. It was one thing to read a lesson from the attack of a mouse upon a prayer book; it was another thing for a woman to prophesy and to set up teachings with which the elders did not agree.

arbitrary monarch; government was established not to make life, liberty, and property less secure but more secure. This is Locke's statement of the case. Thus in the doctrines concerning the origin of government, we find the basis of constitutional principles of the first magnitude, including what the modern lawyers call "constitutional limitations."

Lest it appear that I have been stressing unduly the prevalence of the compact-theory of government, it is desirable to give documentary evidence. The Virginia Bill of Rights of 1776, declared, "That all men are by nature equally free and independent, and have certain inherent rights, of which, when they enter into a state of society, they cannot, by any compact, deprive or divest their posterity; namely, the enjoyment of life and liberty, with the means of acquiring and possessing property, and pursuing and obtaining happiness and safety."[13] New Jersey in 1776 said: "Whereas all the constitutional authority ever possessed by the kings of Great Britain over these colonies, or their other dominions, was, by compact, derived from the people, and held of them, for the common interest of the whole society; . . . And whereas George the Third, king of Great Britain, has refused protection . . . all civil authority under him is necessarily at an end." Maryland declared, "All government of right originates from the people, is founded in compact only, and instituted solely for the good of the whole." Pennsylvania: "All men are born equally free and independent, and have certain natural, inherent and inalienable rights, amongst which are, the enjoying and defending life and liberty, acquiring, possessing and protecting property, and pursuing and obtaining happiness and safety." Jonathan Mason, Jr., of Boston, March 6, 1780, said, "As a reward for our exertions in the great cause of freedom, we are now in the possession of those rights and privileges attendant upon the original state of nature, with the opportunity of establishing a government for ourselves, inde-

---

[13] Over 1500 years before this, Ulpianus said: "Jure enim naturali ab initio omnes liberi nascebantur."

pedent upon any nation or people upon earth."[13A]
In a speech by Thomas Dawes, Jr., in 1781, there is
this declaration: "And yet the people of Massachusetts have reduced to practice the wonderful theory.
A numerous people have convened in a state of nature, and, like *our ideas* of the patriarchs, have
deputed a few fathers of the land to draw up for
them a glorious covenant."[13A]

The constitution of Massachusetts (1780) declares that "The body politic is formed by a voluntary association of individuals: it is a social
compact, by which the whole people covenants with
each citizen, and each citizen with the whole people,
that all shall be governed by certain laws for the common good." In the adoption of the Constitution of
the United States, we find Massachusetts "Acknowl-
edging with grateful hearts the goodness of the
Supreme Ruler of the Universe, in affording the
people of the United States, in the course of his
providence, an opportunity, deliberately and peace-
ably, without fraud or surprise, of entering into an
explicit and solemn compact with each other, by
assenting to the ratifying a new constitution." This
resolution, be it remembered, was passed but eight
years after the State had formed its own constitution
which, as we shall see, was established after the
most careful and thoughtful consideration of the
whole theory of compact and its solemn implications.

In the letter drawn up by the federal Convention
of 1787, and sent with the Constitution to the Congress of the Confederation we find this statement:
"It is obviously impracticable in the federal government of these States, to secure all right of independent sovereignty to each, and yet provide for the
interest and safety of all—Individuals entering into
society, must give up a share of liberty to preserve
the rest."[14] Thus it is plain that the framers of the

[13A] H. Niles, **Principles and Acts of the Revolution in America,**
Baltimore, 1822, 46, 52. Cf. Harry A. Cushing, **History of the Tran-
sition from Provincial to Commonwealth government in Massachusetts,** New York, 1896, 7n.
[14] **Documentary History of the Constitution,** III, 734n.

federal Constitution looked upon it as a sort of social compact among thirteen individual bodies. The Massachusetts people seem to have considered the federal Constitution as a compact entered into by the three million individuals. But if there is conflict between these two assumptions, the fact still remains that the idea of contract, by which a new body-politic was established, furnished the basis of thinking. Coupled with this notion was the thought that this body had authority as long as its action was kept within the power granted by the compact, the fundamental instrument on which union and unity were founded.

For a long time after 1788 and the forming of the federal Constitution, there remained the idea—and I rather think it is still the orthodox idea lying at the basis of constitutional law as announced by the courts—that sovereignty is divided between the state and the nation: just as individuals entering from a state of nature into a state of organized society surrender a portion of their individual rights in order to make the remainder more secure, so states, as separate bodies-politic, may form a new body, to which certain portions of sovereignty are granted, that they may be more safely possessed of their liberty and peace.

Now it is a fact of signal importance that the greatest argumentative controversy in our history, after the formation and adoption of the federal Constitution, was the question whether or not the Constitution was a law binding on the states. Could they, if they should so choose, could any one of them if it so desired, secede from the Union; and did each one have this right because the Constitution was a contract to which the states were parties? Time does not allow any extended comment upon this controversy. But we must take the time to point out that, for an understanding of it, one needs to bear in mind the political philosophy of the eighteenth century, which was as we have seen not new, indeed was centuries old; it was particularly cherished and objectified and acknowledged by the New Englanders in their colonial and religious institutions. It is

equally important to see the entry of a new political
philosophy in the nineteenth century—we may call
it the organic or vital philosophy—which swept aside
the theory and the fundamental thinking of the
whole conception of natural right and the compact
-origin of society. When Calhoun, with a word or
two of contempt, dismissed the announcement that
all men were born equal, or when John Taylor of
Caroline cast aside the doctrine of natural law, he
partly expressed and partly by inference swept aside
also the theory of inherent individual right, and he
also repudiated distinctly the theory that men by
entering into a compact of association could create
a new reality, a new political or social being. If the
Constitution was a compact, then, these men declared, it did not form a new and real body-politic.

I shall make no attempt to defend or attack Calhoun's doctrines. Abstractly considered, taken only
as doctrines of a philosophy to be contemplated so
to speak *in vacuo*—if the philosopher's study or
his brain may be considered even for practical purposes a vacant place—his doctrines are, I suppose,
congenial in the modern atmosphere. No student seriously accepts the social contract as an objective historical reality; probably he does not really accept or
conceive of the existence of an individual who originally was, or at any time could be, a monad float-
ing through space, a man disassociated and ab-
stracted, a being devoid of relationships. But to hold
this it is not necessary to cast aside the theories that
I have attempted to present to you, to ignore them
as if they never had been and need not be taken
into consideration—artificial though they may seem
to be—in the interpretation of American constitutional history.

So much of our constitutional history is the history of words and their connotation that any tendency to ignore the meaning of the words, as that
meaning was held by men of previous generations,
results in misunderstanding of very actual and very
real facts. No other history probably is so interwoven

with ideas concerning the nature of government and the state. This history is peculiarly interlaced with the interpretation of written documents and with declarations about, law, legal obligations, and powers. As arguments, pronouncements, and debates constitute so much of American history, then the connotation of words, as they appeal to men using them, is of the utmost consequence to the historian, whatever may be said of the politician.

The critical question of American constitutional history is whether the Constitution was or was not a compact; at least so, I think, most persons would declare. But, of course, one must place some meaning upon the word "compact," if he is to use it with intelligence. In reality the critical question was, whether the Union was a unity, legally speaking, an indivisible whole. If the Constitution was a compact, was it a binding law and did it create a living legal entity? In 1798, Thomas Jefferson and James Madison drafted the celebrated Kentucky and Virginia Resolutions. The first resolution of the first Kentucky set, declared that the Constitution was a compact to which the states were parties and that the powers of the federal government were limited by the plain sense and intention of the compact.

Madison in the Virginia Resolutions announced a similar principle. Historians interpreting these documents generally, I think, place emphasis upon the word "compact"; and they reach the conclusion that, if the Constitution was a compact, then it did not constitute the fundamental law of state, i.e., the United States was not a body-politic but was a coöperative association of independent sovereignties. But did Madison believe, as a result of the compacting, the states continued essentially independent and remained just as they had been before the compact was made? Did he believe the result of the compact was not the creation of a body-politic or of a binding law? Everything, you see, depends on the connotation of the words. To the men of the eighteenth century there was no more solemn and forceful word than "compact," unless possibly "constitution." Men brought up under the influence of the reigning political philosophy of the time believed that all decent government originated in compact; they were not as yet far removed from Milton's declaration that no one would be so stupid as to deny it. And we must remember too that Jefferson, the author of the Resolutions, was likewise the author of the Declaration of Independence. The fact then would appear to be that when these men declared the states had entered into a compact, they believed that the states as well as the federal government were bound by it.

When South Carolina, in 1832-1833, proceeded to act on the theory elaborately expounded by Calhoun, the senate of Massachusetts in reply spoke as that state might have spoken, as indeed she did speak, forty-five years before: "The Constitution of the United States of America is a solemn Social Compact, by which the people of the said States, in order to form a more perfect union . . . formed themselves into one body politic."[14A] Ohio, which in some respects was the western daughter of New England, "Resolved that the Federal Union exists in a solemn compact, entered into by the voluntary consent of the people of the United States, and of each and every State, and that, therefore, no state can claim the right to secede from, or violate, that compact."[14A] Andrew Jackson put the matter in a nutshell: "Because the Union was formed by compact, it is said the parties to that compact may, when they feel themselves aggrieved, depart from it; but it is precisely because it is a compact that they cannot. A compact is an agreement or a binding obligation.[14A] Plainly enough, if we delve into the merits of the controversy, in its philosophic character, we find one contestant declaring, as Jackson said, that inasmuch as the constitution was a compact it did constitute a binding, legal obligation; his opponents declaring that inasmuch as it was a compact it was not a binding obligation.

As I have already said, it is impossible to discuss this question at length, and I have no disposi-

[14A] **State Papers on Nullification,** Boston, 1834, 128, 206, 87.

tion to attempt to prove or disprove the position of either contestant. But it is perfectly obvious that you cannot interpret and understand the central and pivotal question of American constitutional history, without any knowledge of the meaning of terms, or without any appreciation of the fundamentals of a political philosophy—that is to say, the elements of the way in which people thought about things of that kind. The men of the Revolution, above all the New Englanders, would have been astonished and confounded had anyone told them the result of a compact was not to establish a new unity, to which the parties must be obedient. For the understanding of American history, I began this course of lectures with Robert Browne, the Separatist church, the covenant, though I might have started with a much earlier time, had there been space for considering the whole history of the conception of compact, covenant, and constitutionalism.

There is, however, one other aspect of this topic demanding a moment's consideration. In the nineteenth century we find the announcement or the assumption that a law is the expression of the will of a superior directed to the inferior: inasmuch as the states were *equal* when they ratified the Constitution the Constitution could not be law *ex vi termini*. This question, that is to say whether a law necessarily emanates from a superior, is treated at great length and with remarkable acumen by James Wilson in lectures delivered to the students of the University of Pennsylvania soon after the establishment of the federal Constitution. He had been one of the most effective and able members of the federal Convention, and, when these lectures were delivered, was an associate justice of the Supreme Court. His argument and his analysis are peculiarly significant because they display not only great learning but an unusual philosophic grasp. He was deeply interested in the problems of the nature of law and the foundations of government. Like all other advocates of the doctrine of compact, he resented the notion that government has intrinsic rather than derived power. He saw the theory of superiority damaging to the general conception of the origin of government in the people. He examined with utmost care the statement of Blackstone, "Law is that rule of action which is prescribed by source superior, and which the inferior is bound to obey." This statement when analyzed, he said, implies that government gets its authority from some other *source* than the people who are the subjects of government. He declared this principle to be "subversive of all human law." The result of his discussion was a denial of Blackstone's definition and the philosophy on which it rested. "In one of my lectures," he said, "I proved, I hope, that the only reason, why a free and independent man was bound by human laws, was this— that he bound himself. Upon the same principle on which he becomes bound by the laws, he becomes amenable before the courts of justice, which are formed and authorized by those laws. If one free and independent man, an original sovereign, may do all this; why may not an aggregate of free and independent men, a collection of original sovereigns, do this likewise?"[15]

It is not my intention to assert that Wilson was right or wrong. My desire is to produce one piece of evidence of the way in which the whole philosophy of the compact-origin of the state pointed to the conception of obedience and conformity as the consequent of covenant or consent. There can be no question of the general prevalence of this idea in America of the eighteenth century. Wilson's pronouncement means in brief, that government receives its just authority from the consent of the governed. The New Englander of 1780, when he voted to ratify and establish the state constitution, or later when he participated in establishing the Constitution of the United States—each of which he considered and called a social compact—would have been perplexed had he been told that power, authority, and obedience were not all the fruit of agreement.

[15] Wilson's **Works** (Andrews' edition), II, 153. Cf. also I, 196, where he declares that by the principles of the municipal law of England "a superior is not necessary to the existence of obligation. A man can bind himself."

IV

The Constitutional Convention

IN THE EARLIER lectures, when speaking of the origins of Separatism or of the democratic church, and of the beginnings of trading-companies, corporations, and colonies, I spoke of the creation of a body through the process of the theory of social compact on which all civil bodies-politic were said to rest, a fact which Milton said no one would be so stupid as to deny. I propose now to consider the actual method of setting up states in America, and in doing this to illustrate further the seriousness with which the Fathers viewed the old time-worn doctrines and sought to actualize and objectify the philosophy of association.

All of the states save Rhode Island and Connecticut drew up constitutions; and all these documents were thought of more or less as coming from the people and expressing popular will. These constitutions bear the characteristics and qualities of American constitutionalism. I have already called attention to the celebrated Bill of Rights of Virginia which is in some respects a peculiarly happy expression of the ideas of natural right, social compact, and unchanging principles. Few men in America, even though untouched by Puritan theology or politics—and many of the Southerners had been influenced by these doctrines—would deny these elementary notions. Though the Separatists and their American descendants had given to the principle of association very concrete expression in the churches and explicit pronouncement in their theology, that idea and all its connections were not unfamiliar to men whatever their faith. But I wish to dwell upon

86

New England because that region has been mainly the field of these lectures; I have sought to trace the line of descent or advance of certain constitutional principles, especially through New England history. It is quite plain that the men of the north were more distinctly conscious of their philosophy; at all events they were more articulate in this philosophy than the constitution-makers of other regions.

The process of revolution was the transmutation of colonies into commonwealths. So evidently was this the fact that the leading Revolutionary spirits were eager, even before independence was formally declared, to establish governments capable of managing the affairs of the colonies. The significance of this movement is well illustrated by a remark made by John Adams in a conversation with a fellow member of the old Congress. The subject of discussion was a resolution recommending the states to form constitutions. "Mr. Duane called it to me, a machine for the fabrication of independence. I said, smiling, I thought it was independence itself, but we must have it with more formality yet."[1] The establishment of state governments by the people was the dramatic and conclusive proclamation of independence. The doctrine of the right of revolution, as the doctrine was expressly announced in the Declaration of Independence, included the right of people not only to overthrow a government but to set up a new one, capable of protecting their safety and securing their happiness. The American Revolution deserves distinction among revolutions, not because a monarchy was overthrown, but because of the peaceful skill with which institutions were founded on a lasting basis.

The matter of greatest importance is the way in which the constructive work of the Revolution was accomplished. Gradually, in the course of the year immediately preceding the formal announcement

[1] **Works,** III, 46. Adams declared, "From the beginning, I always expected we should have more difficulty and danger, in our attempts to govern ourselves, and in our negotiations and connections with foreign powers, than from all the fleets and armies of Great Britain." Ibid., III, 13.

of independence, thoughts concerning the foundation of state governments were taking shape; the necessities of the case were becoming plain. The states were in the hands of the revolutionists; the existing governments, differing somewhat from colony to colony, were manifestly temporary. Had the people been less free, less intelligent, and less legal-minded, they might have been content—as revolutionists are inclined to be content with the success of force and the destruction of authority—to go along without more ado, settling down for a time, satisfied with the revolutionary congress and local committees which carried on the war and regulated domestic concerns. They might have shuffled along for years with no anxiety about the establishment of permanent and well-organized government; and, had real revolutionary or destructive spirit gained control, social and economic disorder would in all probability have increased. But the leaders, and the people at large probably, were not willing to rest content. It is a very impressive story, this framing of constitutions in a time of war. The task demanded sobriety of judgment and great political capacity. The story of the accomplishment ought not to be lost amid the blare of trumpets or entirely obscured even by the picture of the valor and the suffering of Washington and the old continentals, that meager and courageous army which struggled often in vain to hold the battle-front.

I think, and have thought for years, that the emphasis which our schoolbooks and all sort of patriotic appeals lay upon the destructive side of the Revolution is unfortunate. To teach our youth and to persuade ourselves that the heroes of the controversy were only those taking part in tea-parties and various acts of violence is to inculcate the belief that liberty and justice rest in the main upon lawless force. And yet as a matter of plain fact, the self-restraint of the colonists is the striking theme; and their success in actually establishing institutions under which we still live was a remarkable achievement. No one telling the truth about the Revolution will attempt to conceal the fact that there was disorder. Anyone knowing the frailties of human nature will understand the seamy side of the period. No one more clearly than Washington characterized and denounced the many evidences of selfishness and the want of high-minded patriotism. It is necessary to read only Washington's own writings to get a fairly clear and comprehensive picture of the demoralizing effect of war and the overthrow of government. But if we examine the whole period of the Revolution from the beginning of the agitation against the Stamp Act to the close of the war and onward till the federal Constitution was established, we find it marked on the whole by constructive political capacity.

We shall never appreciate the Revolution till we recognize and properly evaluate the constructive triumphs and cease to laud the merely destructive tendencies and effects; for it was not enough simply to break the British Empire; the job was to institutionalize principles and to establish firm and effective government. I should like to see the time when the average American citizen will count John Adams among the heroes of the American Revolution, because he was the leader in the task of establishing state governments and drafting state constitutions. If especially at a later time he was too distrustful of popular power, if he did not share with Jefferson the optimistic philosophy which must be the basis of democratic faith, no one can deny to him the credit for high constructive statesmanship.

It is not my purpose to attempt to give a full description of the conditions during the war; but no one can appreciate the actual accomplishments of American statesmanship without some knowledge of the difficulties which were actually surmounted. Without such knowledge the constructive and preservative achievements might seem rather simple; and indeed, we generally take these achievements for granted, as if constitutions, civic order, courts and legislatures, national union, and a sentiment of national partriotism, all came into existence quite easily and without the expenditure of effort and without the exercise of wisdom as well as courage.

In this year when we are all expressing in one way or another our admiration for the man who stands out in unsullied greatness, the one statesman of the world's history whom one can properly revere without qualification, it is well to remember not only his qualities as a general but the influence of his character, when nothing was so much needed as sobriety of judgment. Washington's supreme gift was the gift of patience and calm determination. In private letters he sometimes lamented the disheartening display of greed, avarice, extravagance, and waste; but the impressive fact is not abundance of complaint or fretful protest against the injustice which he and his fellow soldiers were called upon to suffer; the impressive thing is his calm endurance of unnecessary hardship. Fretting inwardly because of the incompetence of Congress and the personal wrangles of politicians, he always assumed toward Congress an air of dignified and courteous deference. How easy it would have been to bring all to naught by explosions of unseemly if justifiable wrath, or by reaching out for power in contemptuous disregard of the men with whom he had to deal. In a time when national patriotism was at a low state, when indeed there appeared at times to be no national patriotism to be built upon, Washington embodied patriotic attachment to the nation, which indeed his own prowess, his own integrity, and his own invulnerable patience were actually creating.

Washington would be the last to assert that military victories alone, rather than the establishment of settled government and peaceful social order, presented in full the task of the American people. Indeed the task of winning independence on the battle field was rendered doubly or trebly difficult by the absence of efficient political institutions, especially national institutions. I speak of these facts, not only, as I have said, as a tribute to Washington, but also as a background for an understanding of the skill and wisdom, with which even in time of war and amid social confusion men did succeed in establishing state institutions, built on those elementary philosophical principles which were the basis of the war and the products of previous thought.

One word from John Adams gives us a picture of one phase of this situation in the early years. Recounting an experience on his way home from a meeting of the old Congress, he says:

"An event of the most trifling nature in appearance, and fit only to excite laughter in other times, struck me into a profound reverie, if not a fit of melancholy. I met a man who had sometimes been my client, and sometimes I had been against him. He, though a common horse-jockey, was sometimes in the right, and I had commonly been successful in his favor in our courts of law. He was always in the law, and had been sued in many actions at almost every court. As soon as he saw me, he came up to me, and his first salutation to me was, 'Oh! Mr. Adams, what great things have you and your colleagues done for us! We can never be grateful enough to you. There are no courts of justice now in this Province, and I hope there never will be another.' Is this the object for which I have been contending? said I to myself, for I rode along without any answer to this wretch. Are these the sentiments of such people, and how many of them are there in the country? Half the nation, for what I know; for half the nation are debtors, if not more, and these have been, in all countries, the sentiments of debtors. If the power of the country should get into such hands, and there is great danger that it will, to what purpose have we sacrificed our time, health, and everything else? Surely we must guard against this spirit and these principles, or we shall repent of all our conduct. However, the good sense and integrity of the majority of the great body of the people came into my thoughts, for my relief, and the last resource was after all in a good Providence."[2]

One other illustration must suffice. Writing to Benjamin Harrison on December 18, 1778, Wash-

[2] **Works,** II, 420-1.

ington spoke freely of certain disheartening conditions as he knew them. It is true that before that time most of the states had established state governments; but his letter nevertheless shows a situation that confronted and often baffled the real statesmen of the time. "If I was to be called upon to draw a picture of the times and of Men, from what I have seen, and heard, and in part know, I should in one word say that idleness, dissipation and extravagance seems to have laid fast hold of most of them. That speculation—peculation—and an insatiable thirst for rishes [sic] seems to have got the better of every other consideration and almost of every order of Men. That party disputes and personal quarrels are the great business of the day whilst the momentous concerns of an empire—a great and accumulated debt—ruined finances—depreciated money—and want of credit (which in their consequences is the want of everything) are but secondary considerations and postponed from day to day—from week to week as if our affairs wear the most promising aspect . . . And yet an Assembly—a concert —a Dinner—or supper (that will cost three or four hundred pounds) will not only take Men off from acting in but even from thinking of this business while a great part of the Officers of the Army from absolute necessity are quitting the service and the more virtuous few rather than do this are sinking by sure degrees into beggary and want."[3]

We must now return to a consideration of the constructive work of the Revolutionary period and attempt to show how the leaders during the storm and stress of war accomplished their purposes. The movement for state government began with a request to Congress, sent by Massachusetts to the Continental Congress in the spring of 1775, asking for "explicit advice respecting the taking up and exercising the powers of civil government, wch we think absolutely necessary for the Salvation of our country." The answer of Congress is significant: Inasmuch as no obedience was due to a governor or lieutenant

[3] George Washington, **Writings,** (W. C. Ford ed.), VII, 301-303.

governor endeavoring to subvert the charter, those officers should be considered as absent and their offices as vacant, and "that, in order to conform, as near as may be, to the spirit and substance of the charter, it be recommended to the provincial Convention, to write letters to the inhabitants of the several places, which are intituled [sic] to representation in Assembly, requesting them to chuse representatives, and that the Assembly, when chosen, do elect counsellors; which assembly and council should exercise the powers of Government, until a Governor, of his Majesty's appointment, will consent to govern the colony according to its charter."[4] This resolution was passed before the battle of Bunker Hill and thirteen months before the Declaration of Independence. Three things stand forth prominently—first, a certain similarity to the process by which the "glorious Revolution" of 1688 had been carried out in England and in Massachusetts; second, the determination to adhere to existing legal forms as far as possible and not to sweep the past aside; and third, to use the method of popular representation as a means of bringing in substantial government.

In the latter part of the year (1775) similar instruction or advice was sent to New Hampshire and certain other colonies; and in the spring of 1776, a general recommendation was made to such of the colonies as had not as yet formed governments sufficient to the "exigencies of their affairs." In the next year or two governments were set up and constitutions were drafted. All this seems so simple, so inconspicuous, so natural, that, as I have suggested, we do not as a rule grasp the fact that this is what gave distinction to the Revolution. If you disagree with this ascription of distinction, it may be well to trace the history of revolutions of other lands. And if you think the whole thing was easy and required no thought and no talent, a study of the American process, much fuller than can be given here, will convince you to the contrary.

At the very beginning, Adams gave advice and

4 Passed June 9, 1775.

counsel. The account of the problem as he presents it in his autobiography is especially telling. His words were written at a later time, and, it may be, are not entirely correct; but they are worth quoting. He said that the case of Massachusetts "was the most urgent, but that it could not be long before every other Colony must follow her example. That with a view of this subject, I had looked into the ancient and modern confederacies for example, but they all appeared to me to have been huddled up in a hurry, by a few chiefs. But we had a people of more intelligence, curiosity, and enterprise, who must be all consulted, and we must realize [i.e., make real] the theories of the wisest writers, and invite the people to erect the whole building with their own hands, upon the broadest foundation. That this could be done only by conventions of representatives chosen by the people in the several colonies, in the most exact proportions. That it was my opinion that Congress ought now to recommend to the people of every Colony to call such conventions immediately, set up governments of their own, under their own authority; for the people were the source of all authority and [the] original of all power. These were new, strange, and terrible doctrines to the greatest part of the members, but not a very small number heard them with apparent pleasure, and none more than Mr. John Rutledge, of South Carolina, and Mr. John Sullivan, of New Hampshire."[5]

Adams tells us of further conversations in Congress. "How can the people institute governments?" he was asked. "By conventions of representatives, freely, fairly, and proportionably chosen," he answered. "When the convention has fabricated a government, or a constitution rather, how do we know the people will submit to it?" "If there is any doubt of that, the convention may send out their project of a constitution, to the people in their several towns, counties, or districts, and the people may make the acceptance of it their own act."[6] These

[5] John Adams, **Works**, (C. F. Adams ed.), III, 16.
[6] Ibid., 20.

words make the actual situation more vivid and
more real than any words of my own could possibly
do. Often before this time men had philosophized
about the origin of government, or they had attacked the tyrant and the usurper and gloated
over the ruins of his power. Now in America men
set out upon the task of establishing institutions and
were not satisfied by simply grinding the relics of
the old beneath their feet. All this is a matter of profound consequence in American history. How could
people form constitutions and establish states? The
answer is, by means of the representative constitutional convention. That institution is America's
basic institution, founded, however, of course on
the people themselves who create the convention
for temporary service.

The word "convention" usually connotes to students the federal Convention of 1787. That was a
formidable body—perhaps the most distinguished
assembly of lawmakers in history—but we must
remember that there were conventions before that
body met. To a considerable degree the nature of
that institution and the philosophy on which it rested had been well threshed out and put into practice.
Moreover, there have been many scores of conventions in this country and a long history of constitution-making since the meeting of the Fathers at
Philadelphia one hundred and forty-five years ago.

The process, then, by which the colonies were
given legal status and governmental form, is a matter of extreme consequence to anyone desiring to
know the basic elements of the American constitutional system. It is impossible here to recount in any
detail the steps taken by the various states of the
Revolutionary time. I propose to say a few words
about Massachusetts, which, after much consideration, framed the last of the strictly Revolutionary
constitutions. In the whole proceeding there was an
attempt, consciously and purposefully, to follow the
philosophy of the "wisest writers." By their words
and acts the constitution-makers of Massachusetts
made actual the theory of the origin of government

in the will of the people. Their leaders, the lawyers, and many men of humble calling were perfectly familiar with the philosophy of politics. The preachers were prominent and persuasive, once again making clear the whole doctrine of natural right and consent of the governed. In words that are essentially similar to the declarations of the seventeenth century one writer said, "A civil Constitution or form of government is of the nature of a most sacred convenant or contract entered into by the individuals which form the society, for which such Constitution or form of government is intended, whereby they mutually and solemnly engage to support and defend each other in the enjoyment of those rights which they mean to retain. That the main and great end of establishing any Constitution or form of government among a people or in society, is to maintain, secure and defend those natural rights inviolate."[7]

In the spring of 1777, the Revolutionary government of Massachusetts recommended the people at the election to empower their representatives to take part in a convention for making a constitution, which should be submitted to the people for adoption. In accordance with this proposal a convention met, passed a constitution, and turned it over to the people. There were various objections, but chief among them was the absence of a bill of rights. And we must remember, a bill of rights laid down the derivative character of government. This constitution was rejected by the people. The whole discussion is of great interest. Among other treatments of the problem the *Essex Result* (1778) is significant. This pamphlet came from the pen of Theophilus Parsons. It is especially interesting because of the literalness with which he states the contractual nature of the whole undertaking of forming and establishing a constitution. "Over the class of unalienable rights," he said, "the supreme power hath no controul, and they ought to be clearly defined and ascertained in a BILL OF RIGHTS, previous to the ratification of any con-

[7] These are the words of Jonas Clark, quoted by Miss Baldwin, op. cit., 138.

stitution."[8] Also, he declares, the Bill of Rights ought to "contain the equivalent every man receives, as a consideration for the rights he has surrendered."[9] Every contract to be binding—a legal principle as fundamental now as it was a century and a half ago—must contain what is called by the lawyers a "consideration"; and we here find Parsons insisting upon this essential element of a contract on which the state and the government rest.

With the rejection of the proposed constitution, the project was taken up anew. The steps taken brought out sharply and distinctly the nature of the whole process of constitution-making, if the theories of the "wisest writers" were to be made real. The existing government, which was recognized as only a temporary government, asked the people if they desired a constitution, and, if they did, would they empower their representatives to summon a convention for the sole purpose of framing one. The towns responded favorably. A convention was chosen, which proceeded to draft a constitution. It was submitted to the people in town-meeting. It was there debated, and the votes and various suggestions were returned to the convention; the results were there tabulated; the constitution was declared adopted; the convention arranged for the inauguration of the new government.[10] In the preamble of the constitution thus established, a body-politic was defined as a "social compact, by which the whole people *covenants* [the italics are mine], with each citizen, and each citizen with the whole people, that all shall

---

[8] **Memoir of Theophilus Parsons,** 367.

[9] Ibid.

[10] Professor S. E. Morison, in an interesting and valuable study, presents the nature of the criticisms of the people, the methods by which the convention proceeded in passing upon the votes and the suggestions of the people, and in deciding that the constitution had been adopted. The method of reaching the conclusion that it had been adopted by two-thirds of the people voting appears to be not beyond criticism, but no article received less than a majority. In conclusion, he says the formation of the constitution was important "because the plain people of the state, in town meeting assembled, were able to point out the principal flaws that time and experience would find in the constitution drafted by John Adams, and adopted by a Convention that included among its members Samuel Adams, James Bowdoin, Theophilus Parsons, John Lowell, George Cabot, and Robert Treat Paine." **The Struggle over the Adoption of the Constitution of Massachusetts,** 1780, in **Proceedings of the Massachusetts Historical Society, L.,** (1917), 353-402.

be governed by certain laws for the common good."

In the light of all this it is not quite appropriate to treat the compact-origin of government and the body-politic as if it were only a nebulous theory used for the purpose of war and revolution. The idea as a practical working-theory was part of the every-day thinking of the men of New England. But that is not all; the pivotal fact is the use of the doctrine as the basis of state-making. It will not do to point to the theory as only a pretense to be used in the days before the war as a weapon of offense when real argument failed. It was made the basic principle of constructive statesmanship.

As already said, the critical matter is the process or method by which the work was done. That method brought out sharply the derivative character of government. The old controversy between the advocates of the divine right of kings and their opponents—a controversy which was responsible for the development and the elaboration of the social-compact idea—turned upon this very vital question: Did government have original and inherent authority, or did it, when instituted, receive its just powers from the consent of the governed? If we accept the principle or assume as a working postulate, that people came before government and that government has only derived power, the battle for limited government is nearly, if not entirely, won, as far as argument can win battles. The method in Massachusetts left nothing to be desired in the way of a practical exposition of the cornerstone of American constitutionalism.

During the discussion in Massachusetts, there was a clear presentation of the nature of a constitutional convention. We see this in a series of resolutions adopted in the town of Concord, at an early day: "Resolved, secondly, that the supreme Legislature, Either in their proper capacity or in Joint Committee are by no means a Body Proper to form and establish a Constitution of [or?] form of government for Reasones following viz—first Because we conceive that Constitution in its proper Idea intends a system of principals [sic] established to secure the subject in the Possession of, and enjoyment of their Rights and Privileges against any encrouchment of the Governing Part. Secondly Because the same Body that forms a Constitution have of Consequence a power to alter it—thirdly Because a Constitution alterable by the Supreme Legislative is no security at all to the subject against encrouchment of the Governing part on any or all their Rights and Privileges."[11] The whole process by which the second convention was chosen and the method by which the constitution was formed and ratified were in conformity with the principles there enumerated.

By following the methods above described, the people of Massachusetts made clear: *first,* the derivative character of government; *second,* that the government cannot destroy or alter the constitution without destroying its own foundation; the constitution is above mere legislative power; *third,* that the government and state are distinct, the former being only the creature and intended to be the servant of the state—the organized body-politic. This distinction between state and government is one of the chief contributions of the American Revolution to practical politics; it is a fundamental principle of American constitutionalism.

If we turn to the other states we find evidence of these principles; but in general the elementary philosophy is not so clearly brought to light by the process actually followed in the framing and establishment of constitutions. New Hampshire, having acted hastily in 1776, followed a few years later the example of Massachusetts. In most of the states the method by which the constitution was formed did not bring out sharply the distinction between law-making and the extraordinary sovereign power of establishing the constitution. They did not make clear and obvious the elementary principle that constitution-making is not a task for inferiors, not a task to be carried out save by the people, the "original of all power," who are entitled to erect the

---

[11] Quoted in an article by Roger Sherman Hoar, "When Concord invented the Constitutional Convention," in the **Boston Evening Transcript,** July 3, 1917.

whole building with their own hands. This variance from strict theory may be accounted for in various ways; but it is at least noteworthy that in New England the full philosophy of compact was given complete and adequate expression; there the derivative character of government was made perfectly plain and the consequent theory that the law-making body is limited by the constitution.[12]

But again we are not justified in supposing the constitutional convention an absolutely novel idea, or an absolutely new invention, when the people of this country began working on the problem of setting up new government on the basis of popular authority. I must repeat my assertion that the work of the American revolutionist was not so much to create something brand new, as to take up the old, and to make old visions real, give dreams a body, transmute hopes into tangible institutions. You cannot in discussion of American history lose sight of the seventeenth century. When the men of the great Rebellion against the Stuarts seemed to have overthrown the monarchy, they were faced by the same problem and actuated by many of the same desires as were the men of the American Revolution. The more radical or advanced leaders, longing for a government of limited authority, even before the execution of Charles, cast about for a method of establishing it. The Agreements of the people, with their restrictions on governmental authority, are well-known, as is also the famous Instrument of Government. The Agreement put forth by the Levellers in 1649, for example, is an evidence of the sim-

[12] During the first two years of the period of establishing state constitutions (1776-1777) "no conventions were assembled solely for the purpose of framing constitutions. . . . In many states during this period there was a strong feeling that no constitution should be adopted until it should have been submitted to and approved by the people, and the New Hampshire constitution of 1776 was strongly objected to because it was not submitted. Resolutions in New York and North Carolina expressed strongly the demand for a popular voice in the approval of constitutions, but here too it is probably the case that the popular participation was less than might have been desired because of the critical condition of affairs and of the necessity for prompt action. Even under these conditions action was taken in a number of states which amounted to an informal submission of constitutions to the people (Maryland, Pennsylvania, North Carolina, South Carolina, 1778), but the proposed Massachusetts Constitution of 1778 is the first instrument of government which was formally submitted to a vote of the people." W. F. Dodd, **Constitutional Convention** in **Cyclopaedia of American Government.** I, 425.

ilarity between the radicals of that day and the constitution-makers of 1780. It declares that all laws made, or that shall run contrary to any part of this Agreement, are hereby made null and void.[13] But perhaps most significant is the proposal made in 1648 for a representative body which should draft a permanent system: "That those persons ought not to exercise any Legislative power, but onely to draw up the foundations of a just Government, and to propound them to the well-affected people in every Country to be agreed to: Which Agreement ought to be above Law; and therefore the bounds, limits, and extent of the peoples Legislative Deputies in Parliament, contained in the Agreement to be drawn up into a formall contract, to be mutually signed by the well-affected people and their said Deputies upon the dayes of their Election respectively . . ."[14]

This proposal contains the fundamental and elementary qualities of a constitutional convention, as they were set forth by the town meeting at Concord nearly a century and a third later. It contains the central idea that the convention is not to legislate, and also the important but less essential declaration that the agreement should be submitted to the people. I do not know that John Adams would have cited John Lilburne, the chief of the Levellers, as one of the "wisest writers"; but one can imagine that the men of Massachusetts were acquainted with the seventeenth-century prophetic picture of a constitutional convention. Whether they were or not so acquainted, they knew the history of the great English Rebellion, and they had well fastened in their minds the logic of the contract-origin of government. It would be strange indeed, if they did not know Sir Henry Vane's *Healing Question,* published in 1656. Vane had been for a brief season a governor of the Massachusetts colony and had gone back to England soon after the decisive victory of Winthrop and the old guard, when they used their power to crush Anne Hutchinson and the Antinomians.

---

[13] Gardiner, S. R., **The Constitutional Documents of the Puritan Revolution,** (Oxford, 1906, 3d ed. rev.), 359-371. The pronouncement refers to the fundamental portions.

[14] T. C. Pease, **The Leveller Movement,** (1916), 261.

Vane's idea of a convention is similar to that of the Levellers and to that of the townsmen of Concord during the American Revolution:

"The most natural way for which would seem to be by a generall councill, or convention of faithfull, honest, and discerning men, chosen for that purpose by the free consent of the whole body of adherents to this cause in the several parts of the nations, and observing the time and place of meeting appointed to them (with other circumstances concerning their election) by order from the present ruling power, but considered as generall of the army.

"Which convention is not properly to exercise the legislative power, but only to debate freely, and agree upon the particulars; that, by way of fundamentall constitutions, shall be laid and inviolably observed as the conditions upon which the whole body so represented doth consent to cast it self into a a civil and politick incorporation, and under the visible form and administration of government therein declared, and to be by each individuall member of the body subscribed in testimony of his or their particular consent given thereunto. Which conditions so agreed (and amongst them an act of oblivion for one) will be without danger of being broken or departed from; considering of what it is they are the conditions and the nature of the convention wherein they are made, which is of the people represented in their highest state of soveraignty . . ."[15]

These extensive quotations are made, not for the purpose of wearying the listener, but to establish beyond all cavil the connection between the earlier and the later movements of rebellion and revolution; both were the work of Englishmen in protesting against illiberal government. There was more than a logical connection; there was, as I have shown, a continuous unbroken line between the religious and political theories of the early seventeenth century on the one hand, and the theories of the New England revolutionists of the eighteenth century on the other. But this mere fact of connection or continuity, this association of rebellion in one century

[15] Somers' Tracts, VI, 312.

with rebellion and revolution in the next, is of no great importance unless it makes clear a simple but profoundly important fact which, in a way, is the burden of my song: institutions of lasting influence are not begotten in a moment, stricken off by an excited populace in a spasm of impatience or of heated idealism. They are the product of slowly working time; and if they are viable, if they actually persist in peace, that persistence is to be attributed to the creative process of history.

It is therefore not merely a piece of antiquarianism, this effort to show the way in which the religious and political theories of an earlier time sifted down through the centuries. We have already noticed that the doctrines set forth in the Declaration of Independence were very old. They had been announced many times before. But that fact should not be taken as the basis for contemptuous reflections. The striking historical fact—as I have sought laboriously to illustrate and demonstrate— is this: the Americans of the Revolutionary period, engaged in the difficult job of establishing institutions in time of war, made those ancient theories, of which they were entirely conscious, into actual institutions. Not therefore because of the invention of the absolutely new, but because of the actualization of the old, the Revolution won its chief distinction and found the basis for continued usefulness. It is an amazing and profoundly impressive fact that this realization—this making of the old into the new and the real—forms the substantial ground on which we stand to-day— even to-day when we question everything. But if there is any lesson to be learned from the whole history of these ideas, it must be that the task of the statesman and of the rest of us is to know the teachings of the past and not to imagine that the past can be impatiently torn up by the roots and cast upon the refuse heap. Historians will probably tell you this: the principles and the practices, which have shown special vitality in our constitutional system, are those which were the fruit of experience and the product also of long and sustained desire.

V

The Courts and the Right of Judicial Review; The Reign of Law

In the last lecture, I discussed the method by which constitutions were framed in the Revolutionary days. That method, especially in New England, was in accord with the fundamental doctrine of the social-compact philosophy. We saw that the theoretical and practical principle involved the idea that a government is inferior to the state, and that the document on which the legislative power rested is the warrant of legislative authority. I now wish to make clear this principle of American constitutionalism; and first it may be well to begin with a brief expression of it, as we know it to-day, and then return to the history and thus see how it found permanent lodgment in American law.

If there is any central principle in the American constitutional system, it is that governments are not omnipotent; they are, or are supposed to be, of only limited authority. This principle of limited authority is sometimes spoken of as the reign of law. Liberty has been often defined as the right or the privilege of not being under restraint or obligation to obey anything but the law.[1] The struggle for freedom in English history was largely directed against arbitrary government, against a system or a ruler with power

---

[1] "The liberty o. nan in society is to be under no other legislative power but that established by consent in the commonwealth, nor under the dominion of any will, or restraint of any law, but what that legislative shall enact according to the trust put in it." Locke's **Two Treatises, . . . An Essay Concerning the True Original, Extent, and End of Civil Government,** Sect. 22. This statement of Locke's does not fully express the idea of a government which is itself bound by law; but his whole argument is against arbitrary and unrestrained government.

to act capriciously and with no responsibility to the governed. The long course of history during which men cherished the hope, often only a hope, of living under legally limited government is an impressive story. It is for us especially impressive, because the American people, a century and a half ago, succeeded in establishing that principle as an institutional fact; and the climax of the age-long effort for freedom from a capricious government was found in the full recognition of the principle that a governmental act beyond the border of assigned authority is not law. In the present condition of American society, one finds peculiar interest in the fact that so many centuries of hope and effort have been directed to the establishment of a system wherein governments will obey law; and now the pressing problem appears to be whether men will pay decent obedience to government.

We all know that the courts use the power of declaring a legislative act void. This is done because it is the duty of courts to announce and apply the law in controversies. Questions of constitutional importance often, though not always, arise in suits between two ordinary citizens, each asking for justice according to law at the hands of the court. This duty of the courts and their activity are often spoken of as if it were a peculiar function of the federal courts in passing upon the validity of federal legislation. But to single out the federal judiciary or the federal Constitution leads to a primary misunderstanding. The first thing to be noticed is this: when a court of any jurisdiction—federal or state—passes upon a controversy involving the question of constitutionality, it does just what it is accustomed to do in all other cases. There is no special and peculiar procedure, no anomalous principle; for the court's duty is to announce the law and to decide controversies according to law. That is what courts are for. Whether the suit be between plain John Doe and Richard Roe and the question has arisen about the binding character of a contract for the sale of a plow-horse, or about matters which involve the character

and effect of legislative enactment, anything contrary to law, cannot be legal; and if Congress or a
state legislature go beyond the law its act is not law.

In the second place, this principle and practice,
this authority to declare legislative acts not to be law,
was not only first exercised by state courts, but has
been used there with great freedom for about a
hundred and fifty years, and more and more frequently as the decades have gone by, because of the
multitude of acts passed by state legislatures. State
acts in literally thousands of cases have been pronounced void, not law, by state courts, because those
acts violated the state constitution. It is, therefore,
nothing less than amusing to see the heavy artillery
of criticism trained upon the federal courts, as if
they were the main malefactors and usurpers of
authority, who seized upon power and are wantonly
exercising it. As a matter of fact, before the Civil
War, there were only two cases in which a Congressional act was pronounced void by the federal
Supreme Court.[2] There, is, I must admit, serious
question whether in either case the Court was fully
justified in making such decision. But that question
is just now of no importance.

In the third place—and this fact is perhaps suffici-
ently indicated by the paragraph above—the courts
do not set themselves up as a special umpire, exercising a special function, or as a superior dictating
to the legislative body. If we should examine carefully the early state decisions, we should find the
courts announcing their independence, their independent right to find and declare the law. In other
words their right to ignore an act contrary to the
Constitution was based on the principle of the separation of the powers of government.

Let us now turn to the historical antecedents of
limited government, the sources from which the idea
and the principle arose. I propose to pay no special
attention to the history of England from the day
when King John met the famous assembly at Runny-

[2] Marbury v. Madison in 1803, (1 Cranch 137); The Dred Scott
Case, 1857, (19 Howard 393).

mede, though that history is of great importance to
us. My purpose is to associate the principle with the
subject presented in the earlier lectures: the idea of
individual rights which are not created by government or society but exist in a state of nature before
governments are instituted; the idea and principle of
the social compact, the origin of political order in
agreement, the idea that government rests on the
consent of the governed. The belief in the law of
nature, antedating society and permanent in its obligation, is a very old belief; it can be found, as we
have seen, in ancient Roman philosophy. It played
a very important rôle through the whole history of
political philosophy. Five hundred years before the
Declaration of Independence, Thomas Aquinas said
substantially this: "Every human law has just so
much of the nature of law, as it is derived from the
law of nature. But if in any point it deflects from the
law of nature it is no longer a law; it is but a perver-
sion of law."[3] This sounds very modern, if we
supplant the words "law of nature" by the word
"constitution." And this statement is not essentially
different from Locke's declaration: "The law that
was to govern Adam was the same that was to govern all his posterity, the law of reason."[4] No American legislative act to-day can lawfully deprive any
person of his life, liberty, or property, without "due
process of law"—that is to say, it cannot arbitrarily
and unjustly so deprive him. No act of government
in America is held valid in the courts which is believed by the court to be in violation of the elementary principles of substantial justice. Against such
deprivation, the fifth and fourteenth amendments to
the federal Constitution are directed.

The social-compact philosophy was emphatic in
its doctrine that government rested on consent; and
an immediate consequence of this consent was the
responsibility of government. The larger part of

---

[3] **Summa Theologica,** Part II. Third No., (1915 ed.), Q. 95, art. 2,
p. 57 (translated by the English Dominican Province).

[4] Locke, op cit., Sect. 57 Thomas Aquinas quotes Augustine as
saying, "A law that is not just seems no law at all." **Summa Theologica,** Part II, Third number, (1915 ed.), Q. 96, art. 4, p. 70.

Locke's treatise, already referred to, is to demonstrate that men would not come out of a state of nature, in which they existed free and equal, in order to put themselves in bondage to a government able to act arbitrarily and without restraint save that of its own will. Thus the whole character and quality of governmental authority was permeated with the idea that it was not irresponsible and that it was limited by the plain purposes of the compact on which security rests.

I must allow myself a repetition of some essential principles. To the Puritans, the law of nature, the law which Locke and other philosophers postulated as existing before government and social order were founded—this law which was all inclusive and permanent—inevitably assumed religious or theological significance. The law of nature was the law of God as well as the law of reason; and God himself was the embodiment of unchanging reason and inviolable law. I have already referred to the theological belief that God treated with man in a covenant way. But man's hope for salvation was based on the binding character of God's convenant; and He who was the source of right and justice could not, because of His very nature, prove faithless to His own obligations. The universe under God was a constitutional universe; the monarch of the world was a constitutional monarch, ruling in accord with his own promises and in accord with unvarying justice. If then men longed for a government of law and not of men, they found the principle within their own theology and the basis of their belief was founded in their own faith. Puritanism, so far as it was embodied in American constitutional structure and doctrine, would point to God in His heaven, sovereign over the countless millions of men, bound by contract, bound by reason, and limited by immutable law.[5]

[5] There were certain or uncertain variations in their theology. Cf. Miss A. M. Baldwin's **The New England Clergy and the American Revolution,** Chap. II. But men believing the contractual relationship between men and God must have had great difficulty in believing in God's readiness to break the contract or to disregard the law of reason and justice.

This notion of immutable law was, as I have already suggested, not confined to Puritans alone or embraced solely within their theological and political thinking. On this subject one further word may be necessary. Grotius, whose writings were of great influence, taught that political law should be in accord with natural law. Mr. Gooch speaks of him as one who found the origin of natural law in human nature, in right reason, and in the will of God, who maintains that God Himself cannot change it, and believes that its tenets may be discerned with hardly less precision by the mind than external objects by the senses.[6]

Permit me to break in upon my treatment of earlier history, to call your attention to the elementary principle, which is fully established in the American constitutional system, the principle that men have rights which are not the gift of government, rights which are constitutionally protected. This principle we should notice, is the same as, or substantially similar to, the theory in accordance with which men were viewed as possessed of full freedom in a state of nature. One illustration must suffice here. In 1875, the Supreme Court of the United States was called upon to consider the validity of bonds issued by the city of Topeka to aid a company in founding a factory. The Court declared there could be no lawful tax which is not laid for a public purpose. Justice Miller giving the opinion and the decision of the court said, "The theory of our governments, state and national, is opposed to the deposit of unlimited power anywhere. The executive, the legislative, and the judicial branches of these governments are all of limited and defined powers. There are limitations on such power which grow out of the essential nature of all free governments. Implied reservations of individual rights, without which the social compact could not exist, and which are respected by all governments entitled

---

[6] George P. Gooch, **English Democratic Ideas in the Seventeenth Century,** (1898), 56. Grotius of course was not an Englishman; but his writings were influential wherever men thought seriously about government.

to the name."[7] Rights, then, existed before government.

I must try to make clear the fact that such a pronouncement had for its support a long course of history. We are inclined in this country to look at a few words in a document and to think that the words created the principle which they announce; and we are likely to be ignorant of the aspiration and effort of preceding centuries which actually produced the doctrine that we may use it. It is not necessary to go back many centuries in the history of English law or to examine minutely the struggles for the recognition of the principle in the English constitutional system. Let us be content once more with the seventeenth century.

Before the Long Parliament and the actual rebellion, the leaders combating the theories of absolutism argued from English law and history that the king in the exercise of authority was circumscribed by law. And in the seventeenth century the mingling of religion and practical politics with active rebellion against objectionable government is the conspicuous fact. In his argument concerning the validity of ship-money (1637), St. John declared: "The Law of England, for the applying of that Supreme Power which it hath settled in His Majesty to the particular causes and occasions that fall out, hath set down Methods and known Rules which are necessary to be observed. . . . His Majesty is the Fountain of Bounty; but a Grant of Lands without Letters Patents transfers no Estate out of the King to the Patentee, nor by Letters Patents, but by such words as the Law hath prescribed. His Majesty is the Fountain of Justice; and though all Justice which is done within the Realm flows from this Fountain, yet it must run in certain and known Channels."[8]

---

[7] Loan Assoc. v. Topeka, 20 Wal. (U. S.), 655, 663. It is amusing and interesting to see Justice Johnson of the Supreme Court making in 1810 a declaration which is permeated by the doctrines I have earlier discussed. Chief Justice Marshall decided the case in question upon the contract clause of the Constitution. Johnson was not content: "I do not hesitate to declare that a state does not possess the power of revoking its own grants. But I do it on a general principle, on the reason and nature of things: a principle which will impose laws on the Deity." Fletcher v. Peck, 6 Cranch, 87, 143.

[8] Rushworth, J., **Historical Collections**, II, 484-485, (folio edition).

Those of us who would value aright the principle which has been especially established in the American constitutional system, the principle that law prescribes the limits of government, cannot fail to be impressed, I was about to say affected, by the bold words of the sturdy St. John two hundred and ninety-five years ago. But that was exactly the time when on this side of the ocean the settlers around Boston harbor were beginning a demand for laws limiting the discretion of their own government. "The deputies having conceived great danger to our state, in regard that our magistrates for want of positive laws, in many cases, might proceed according to their discretions, it was agreed that some men should be appointed to frame a body of grounds of laws, in resemblance to a Magna Charta, which, being allowed by some of the ministers, and the general court, should be received for fundamental laws."[9] From this demand, there came before long the famous Body of Liberties, a compound of Magna Charta, the scriptures, and sundry other ingredients. The code was enacted by the general court, and it was wanting, therefore, in one essential quality of a modern constitution—though we should notice that the general court was by the charter possessed of the full power of the corporation—but it illustrated the tendency and the desire for a government of standing law; it manifests a state of mind. It may be associated in our own minds with the statement of Pym in parliament not far from the same time: "All our Petition is for the Laws of *England,* and this Power seems to be another distinct Power from the Power of the Law: I know how to add Sovereign to his Person, but not to his Power: and we cannot leave to him a Sovereign Power: Also we never were possessed of it."[10] Thus according to Pym even parliament was not the possessor of unlimited authority.

We must bear in mind the interest with which the Puritans of Massachusetts watched the contest in England. New England was the child of the

---

[9] **Winthrop's Journal** (Hosmer's edition), I, 151. See also ibid., 323-24; II, 48-49. Winthrop's first statement is made under date of 1635; the second, 1639. The Body of Liberties was enacted in 1641.

[10] Rushworth, **Historical Collections,** I, 562, May, 1628.

seventeenth century; it continued to cherish the doc-trines and exemplify the principles of the English rebellion, long after the Restoration and the apparent failure of the Radical and Puritan cause. There was not much in the fundamental political theory of the American Revolution (particularly as announced in New England) that you cannot find proclaimed in the English Rebellion of the century before. Take for example that proposal already referred to which was made in 1648, for a convention to draw up the "foundations of just Government . . . Which Agreement ought to be above Law; and therefore the bounds, limit, and extent of the people's Legisla-tive Deputies in Parliament"[11]—a fundamental law which is to be superior to all Parliamentary legisla-tion. Or notice the words of Milton, "Therefore when the people, or any part of them, shall rise against the king and his authority, executing the law in any thing established, civil or ecclesiastical, I do not say it is rebellion, if the thing commanded though established be unlawful."[12] And here is an Ameri-can illustration announced about the same time: Roger Williams in his *Bloudy Tenent* declares the sovereign original and foundation of civil power lies in the people, and they may establish governments to suit their condition; this being so, it is evident, he says, that such governments as are created have "no more power, nor for no longer time, than the civil power, or people consenting and agreeing, shall betrust them with."[13] This is the gist, the heart and center of American constitutionalism.

We may now turn again to John Locke, whose words have already been quoted to show he based his theories, as did others, on the original freedom of men and on their association through compact. He went, however, beyond the naked compact, and found in English common law the principle that a person was not bound by the unlawful act of another and could resist unlawful attack upon his person

[11] The Clarke Papers, (Camden Society), II, 258.
[12] Tenure of Kings and Magistrates, Prose Works, (Griswold ed.), I, 387.
[13] Hanserd Knollys Society edition, London, 1848, 214-215.

or property. We must notice carefully that the right of resistance is the right to oppose *unlawful* authority. He then connects the fundamental principle of the common law with the right to resist even the monarch, though he lays special emphasis on the right to oppose the agents of the monarch, the administrative officers attempting under color of office to do an illegal act: "As in some countries the person of the prince by the law is sacred, and so whatever he commands or does, his person is still free from all question or violence, not liable to force, or any judicial censure or condemnation. But yet opposition may be made to the illegal acts of any inferior officer or other commissioned by him, unless he will, by actually putting himself into a state of war with his people, dissolve the government, and leave them to that defence, which belongs to every one in the state of Nature. . . . For the king's authority being given him only by the law, he cannot empower any one to act against the law, or justify him by his commission in so doing."[14] "Whosoever in authority exceeds the power given him by the law . . . ceases in that to be a magistrate, and acting without authority may be opposed, as any other man who by force invades the right of another . . . He that hath authority to seize my person in the street may be opposed as a thief and a robber if he endeavours to break into my house to execute a writ, notwithstanding that I know he has such a warrant and such a legal authority as will empower him to arrest me abroad. And why this should not hold in the highest, as well as in the most inferior magistrate, I would gladly be informed."[15] This is a maxim of the common law which is firmly embodied in American constitutional law; no one under the guise of official authority can trespass upon your constitutional rights; if he has no constitutional authority, if the act which he attempts to enforce is beyond the constitutional authority of the legislative, he is individually responsible for the wrong he does you.

[14] **Two Treatises of Civil Government,** (Morley ed.), Sec. 205, 206.
[15] Ibid., Sec. 202.

It is a principle of English and American law that every man is responsible for his own torts; he cannot plead in justification the orders of a superior or a principal. And if one would appreciate the idea fully, he should notice that this individual responsibility finds full expression in the fact that an official, charged with trespass on the rights of a person, is not brought before a special court, but before a court of ordinary common-law jurisdiction, and the suit is there conducted along the same lines as a suit would be if the controversy were between plain John Doe and Richard Roe, between a fishmonger and a cobbler. When we see this, we see at least one reason why it was comparatively easy, when once the constitution of a commonwealth is recognized as law, for a court to take the tremendous responsibility of declaring even a *legislative* act void, an act for the execution of which an official acting under the guise of authority may be held individually responsible. I may venture to ask you again to bear in mind not so much the complicated institutional system, but the elementary fact, that no person is under obligation to obey what is not law. When the rights of an individual citizen are affected by an act, which he believes to be unconstitutional, he has the right, and indeed we may say the duty, to challenge its validity, in order that the question may be decided by the court.

Several times in the course of these lectures we have come face to face with one principle after another, which happens to be elementary and to be of cardinal importance; they all as a matter of fact emanate, at least in theory, from the assertion of original individual right and from the principle that the people are the source of power. But the one just mentioned deserves particular attention, because, on the basis of this principle, the individual right and the binding effect of constitutional limitatons are made real. We do not bring suits, because of unlawful injury, against judges, or governors, or legislatures, charging them with violation of the constitution of state or nation, but against the administrative officer attempting to carry out the law. No one has the legal authority to act illegally; an officer of a state, seeking to execute an unconstitutional law, cannot clothe himself in the garments of sacred authority; he is in fact a private trespasser; he can in some instances be opposed and in all can be haled before a court and made to respond in damages for the injury inflicted. In our constitutional history there was for a time serious question about the interpretation and effect of the Eleventh Amendment which declares that the federal courts shall not entertain a suit by a citizen against a state.[16] But John Marshall over a hundred years ago laid down the main doctrine in accord with the principles I have just called to your attention: if you bring a suit against a state officer seeking to carry out an unconstitutional act, the suit is not against the state but against the person acting beyond the scope of his authority.

In this way the courts recognized fully in constitutional law the very old maxim of the common law. By this principle they have maintained our constitutional system as a body of law. It is very interesting—is it not?—to see the elements of this doctrine announced in the seventeenth century and used as weapons against the Stuart kings, and to see the intimate relationship between compact and constitutional law. For once more, though we should pay full deference to the history of the early centuries, we find in the seventeenth century in England and America the plain insistence upon the principle as a constitutional principle based upon the theory of derivative government.

The phrase "right of revolution" is known to you all. It deserves much more careful examination than can be given here. I wish to discuss it in connection with the principles which have just been presented. In the thinking of the compact-philosophy as Locke summed it up, the right to resist a monarch was announced in opposition to the theory of passive obedience; but that right existed when the king went *beyond the law*. It did not rest with the people in any fit of petulant discontent to overthrow

---

[16] The words here given are not an exact transcription of the Amendment. But see Hans v. Louisiana, 134 U. S. I.

government; they could resent unlawful action, and, if worse came to worse, depose the king because he had broken the law. You will notice how this emphasizes the character of government as the men of the seventeenth century conceived it; even revolution was in defence of law. And we should mark this carefully, because we shall see in a moment how this doctrine permeated the thinking of the American Revolution and helped to bring into unmistakable prominence the idea that governments to be safe must keep within the confines of assigned authority. We find Thomas Jefferson in the Declaration of Independence justifying the overthrow of King George because he had given his consent to "acts of pretended legislation" and because he had degenerated into a tyrant, using the word "tyrant" presumably as Locke used it, meaning one in authority who has gone beyond the law to the injury of his people; for some of Jefferson's phrases are exact quotations from Locke.

Lest you think this doctrine had not survived in America or was put forth by the American revolutionists as something novel, let us look at some fairly early declarations. In 1744 a New England minister made the announcement that subjects and rulers are bound by the constitution, and that a law violating natural and constitutional rights is no law and requires no obedience.[17] In 1765 Stephen Johnson in his Fast Day Sermon said, "It is a flagrant absurdity to suppose a free constitution empowers any to decree or execute its own destruction: For such a militating self-repugnancy in a constitution necessarily carries its own destruction in it."[18] If we go a little farther along, we find John Lathrop in 1774 referring to the sacredness and inviolability of original compacts. They lie, he declares, "in the foundation of all civil societies" and they "may not be disturbed." "A single article may not be altered

---

[17] Alice M. Baldwin, **The New England Clergy and the American Revolution**, 68.

[18] Ibid., 101. This quotation shows that in all probability the speaker was familiar with the words of Vattel, which will be referred to later. Vattel declared a legislature could not violate the fundamental law without destroying its own foundation.

but with the consent of the whole body.—Whoever makes an alteration in the established constitution, whether he be a subject or a ruler, is guilty of treason. Treason of the worst kind: Treason against the state."[19] And Jonas Clark, in the election sermon of 1781, said: "While the social compact exists, the whole state and its members are bound by it; and a sacred regard ought to be paid to it. No man, party, order, or body of men in the state have any right, power, or authority to alter, change, or violate the social compact. Nor can any change, amendment, or alteration be introduced but by common consent."[20] If this worthy divine had had at his command further synonyms by which to express the idea of unchangeable character of fundamental law, he would doubtless have used them.

It is necessary to quote such words as these to mark the folly of protesting against the courts as usurpers of authority when they exercise the power to proclaim void legislative acts that are in clear violation of the constitution. My purpose is to make abundantly clear how thoroughly the minds of the men of the Revolution, especially the minds of the New Englanders who were taught by their preachers, were saturated, when our constitutions were framed, with the belief that rebellion against illegal authority was no rebellion and that the foundations of the state must remain unviolated. On the basis of the intense and mastering belief that illegal authority was no authority at all, the courts in America were ready to take up the theory and, in protection of law and liberty, use it, when legislatures exercised unlawful power.

The most striking example of the whole theory of law as a limit upon government and of the right to oppose unlawful authority is Jonathan Mayhew's *Discourse Concerning Unlimited Submission,* published in Boston in 1750 and said on the title-page to be the substance of a sermon delivered on the Lord's day after the thirtieth of January, 1749-50. The preface says it is the last of three discourses on

19 Ibid., 181.
20 Ibid., 180.

the same subject. "It was the near approach of the
thirtieth of January [the hundredth anniversary of
the execution of Charles I] that turned my thoughts
to this subject: on which solemnity, the slavish doctrine of passive obedience and non-resistance, is
often warmly asserted ..."

Mayhew scouted the idea that the great rebellion
of the seventeenth century was a rebellion at all.
The king had broken the law and degenerated into
a tyrant; "and now, is it not perfectly ridiculous to
call resistance to such a tyrant, by the name of
rebellion?" Charles, he maintains "had, in fact, *unkinged* himself long before, and had forfeited his
title to the allegiance of the people." Special attention may be paid also to the announcement that "as
soon as the prince sets himself up above law, he
loses the king in the tyrant." No one has the right
"to exercise a wanton licentious *sovereignty* over
the properties, consciences and lives of all the people:—Such a *sovereignty* as some inconsiderately
ascribe to the Supreme Governor of the world.—I
say, inconsiderately; because God himself does not
govern in an absolutely arbitrary and despotic manner. The power of this Almighty King (I speak it
not without caution and reverence; the power of this
Almighty King) is *limited by law;* not indeed, by
acts of Parliament, but by the eternal *laws* of truth,
wisdom and equity; and the everlasting *tables* of
right reason." "Now it is evident, that king Charles's
government was illegal, and very oppressive, through
the greatest part of his reign: And, therefore, to
resist him, was no more rebellion, than to oppose
any foreign invader, or any other domestic oppres-
sor."[21]

    [21] Mayhew, op. cit., reprinted Boston, 1818, v, 41, 41n, 42, 42n.
Cf. Locke, **Two Treatises . . . An Essay Concerning the True Original, Extent, and End of Civil Government,** Sect. 22, 135, 142. This
conception of the rule or reign of law was, of course, similar to the
conception of the existence of a rigid or unchanging constitution.
Perhaps it may be said the two were in logical content identical,
though Locke in his declamation favoring a "standing rule to live
by," does not quite clearly present the idea. "The law of Nature,"
he says, "stands as an eternal rule to all men, legislators as well as
others." He does not use the word constitution; and though the
eternal law of nature is binding, the "established laws" appear to
be the promulgations of the legislators. The legislative power, is to
"govern by promulgated established laws, not to be varied in particular cases, but to have one rule for rich and poor, for the favour-

These words from the New England divine
not reproduce the thinking of theology and
the principles of seventeenth-century opposition to
the divine right of kings; they also introduced us to
the central principle of the American Revolution—
rebellion against an unlawful act is not rebellion but
the maintenance of law. This philosophy gave character to the Revolution. If the colonists had argued,
in the ten years of controversy before the war began, that, while Parliament had the legal right to
tax them, they would not obey, the whole atmosphere of the time would have been essentially different; but in fact, despite outbreaks of angry strife and
occasional vociferous denunciation, the colonists in
their arguments, the really creative arguments, stood
fast by the assertion that Parliament, and at a later
day the king, had gone beyond the law.

In 1761, the famous Writs of Assistance case
arose in Massachusetts. The speech which James
Otis delivered before the colonial court, in which
he condemned the writ as illegal, has been often referred to. John Adams, then a young lawyer, was
present at the argument and from him we gather
practically all we know concerning the words of the
eloquent barrister. Fifty-seven years afterwards,
Adams, in a long letter to Tudor, the biographer of
Otis, described the scene and attempted to give the
content of the speech. But this post-mortem discourse is of little value; we are justified in believing
that Adams's account was a compound of the whole
Revolutionary argument as it developed after 1761,
with occasional intrusions of the writer's own later

---

ite at Court, and the countryman at plough." And still his main
thesis is that by the original compact, men did not surrender to the
monarch or to the legislature arbitrary authority; his whole contention was against the legitimacy of absolute, i.e., unrestrained, government: and though he was writing chiefly to uphold the Parliament against an absolute monarch, he concluded that even the
legislature, in a critical case, need not be obeyed if faithless to the
trust imposed in it. It is sometimes said that Locke mentions no
contract between king or government and the people. In a way that
is true; he was not so explicit as some of the philosophers of a
later day, or indeed, in at least one respect, so explicit as the Parliamentarian of 1688. But his idea is that when men set up government by agreement they did not purpose the creation of an arbitrary, unlimited and capricious government, and that this purpose,
in the very nature of the system, was a guiding principle and constituted a check upon authority.

ruminations. The notes which he took at the time, however, though brief are illuminating. If, as Adams said at a later day, then and there the child of independence was born, the birth was associated with a declaration by Otis against disregard of the traditional privileges of Englishmen, and against the authority of Parliament itself to violate the fundamental principles of English constitutionalism. He in reality proclaimed that England—and, with Englishmen, the colonists—had a fixed constitution, not to be vacated in essentials by Parliamentary statute; in other words, assigning to England the possession of a fixed constitution, he was announcing doctrines which were to be fully and concretely made real in American institutions by that generation. The most important words of Otis, as jotted down in condensed form by Adams, are as follows, "As to Acts of Parliament. An act against the Constitution is void; an act against natural equity is void; and if an act of Parliament should be made, in the very words of this petition, it would be void. The executive Courts must pass such acts into disuse. 8 Rep. 118 from Viner. Reason of the common law to control an act of Parliament."[22] There is nothing more noteworthy than this in American constitutional history. We find there a cardinal principle; the Americans in resisting the authority of England were prepared to assert that they as Englishmen were entitled to the protection of a fixed constitution.

Otis plainly connected natural right—natural equity he calls it—with the fundamental principles of the English constitution. But as a lawyer arguing his case at the bar of a court he cited legal precedent; he referred to an opinion of Coke, in which that famous justice of the early seventeenth century said, "It appeareth in our books, that in many cases the common law will control Acts of Parliament and adjudge them to be utterly void; for where an Act of Parliament is against common right and reason or repugnant or impossible to be performed, the common law will control it and adjudge it to be

[22] John Adams, **Works**, II, 522.

void."[23] Coke had in mind the elementary liberties enshrined, or supposed to be enshrined, in the body of the common law, which was no enactment of Parliament, but was the product of time, and arose in a period when the memory of man runneth not to the contrary. Governor Thomas Hutchinson, writing from Massachusetts in the days when the Stamp Act was assailed, said, "The prevailing reason at this time is, that the Act of Parliament is against Magna Charta, and the natural Rights of Englishmen, and therefore, according to Lord Coke, null and void."

Now, it is not of very much consequence whether such pronouncements were sound and legally valid or not. The fact of consequence is that Otis could cite the words of Coke and that every lawyer knowing English legal history could find in the law-books assertions to sustain his position that there were actual limits on the authority of government. Ascribing to England the possession of a fixed constitution bounding governmental authority, the Americans were at the same time finding a legal basis for opposing Parliament and laying down the elementary characteristics of American constitutionalism.

A county court on the eastern shore of Virginia actually pronounced the Stamp Act unconstitutional and directed that it need not be obeyed.[24] In Massachusetts, Adams and Otis making pleas to the governor in council asked that the courts of justice

[23] The most careful discussion of the Writs of Assistance case is given in I. Quincy Reports (Mass.), where Horace Gray in an appendix discusses the matter with learning. Lord Hobart, it may be noticed, said, "Even an Act of Parliament made against natural equity . . . is void in itself: for jura naturae sunt immutabilia, and they are Leges Legum." And, Lord Holt is reported to have said, "What my Lord Coke says in Dr. Bonham's case in his 8 Rep., is far from any extravagancy, for it is a very reasonable and true saying, That if an Act of Parliament should ordain that the same person should be party and judge, or what is the same thing, judge in his own cause, it would be a void Act of Parliament."

[24] The case referred to in which the Stamp Act was declared void is reported as follows: "Williamsburg, March 21. The following is a copy of a late order of Northampton Court, on the eastern Shore of this colony, which we are desired to insert. Virginia sc. At a court held for Northampton county, Feb. 11, 1766.

"On the motion of the Clerk, and other Officers of this Court, praying their opinion whether the act entitled, 'An act for granting and applying certain Stamp Duties, and other Duties, in America, &c.,' was binding on the inhabitants of this colony, and whether they the said Officers should incur any penalties by not using stamped paper, agreeable to the directions of the said act, the Court

should be allowed to go on without reference or deference to the Stamp Act. That Act, said Adams, "I take it, is utterly void, and of no binding force upon us; for it is against our Rights as Men and our Privileges as Englishmen. An act made in defiance of the first principles of Justice . . . There are certain Principles fixed unalterably in Nature." The able and clever pamphlet which James Otis wrote and published in opposition to the Revenue Act, a pamphlet of peculiar value and interest, contains an elaborate defence of this doctrine of limited governmental powers and of the duty of courts to guard the confines of authority.

In connection with this pamphlet of Otis (*The Rights of the British Colonies Asserted and Proved*) were printed certain instructions of the Boston town-meeting to the town deputies in the general court. These instructions bear on the validity of Parliamentary legislation. The pamphlet (in the edition which I have examined) contained a memorial transmitted by the Massachusetts house to their agent in Britain. There we find quotations from Vattel, a Swiss publicist, whose volume, *The Law of Nations,* was translated into English and published in 1760. It had much influence and was often referred to not only in the latter half of the eighteenth century but the nineteenth as well. Vattel was not an originator of new ideas; but Otis and the Boston town-meeting found in his pages a substantial support of the principles that they wished to present and that we have found associated with covenant, compact, and theology, and also with certain developments of English legal and political history. Speaking of the legislative power in a state, Vattel declares it must "consider the fundamental laws as sacred, if the nation has not, in very express terms, given them power to

unanimously declared it to be their opinion that the said act did not bind, affect, or concern the inhabitants of this colony, in as much as they conceive the same to be unconstitutional, and that the said several officers may proceed to the execution of their respective offices without incurring any penalties by means thereof; which opinion this court doth order to be recorded. Griffin Stith, C.N.C." (Copy) From the **Virginia Gazette.** March 21, 1766. The early cases are briefly summarized in A. C. McLaughlin, **The Courts, The Constitution and Parties,** (Chicago, 1912).

change them. For the constitution of the state ought to possess stability." "In short," he goes on to say, "it is from the constitution that those legislators derive their power: how then can they change it, without destroying the foundation of their own authority?"[25]

Now such words as these, even though given in a pamphlet which must have had wide circulation, we might pass by without especial attention, were it not that the same sort of statement was made in various letters drawn up by the Massachusetts house in 1768. These letters substantially similar one to the other were sent to prominent British statesmen. One letter containing the leading assertions was the famous "circular letter" to the speakers of other houses of representatives in the colonies; it must have been known from one end of the land to the other. Though in a few years some of the colonists were prepared to deny that Parliament had any authority over the colonies, a theory which began to gain currency about 1773, the circular letter and some of the other letters explicitly acknowledge the supreme legislative power of Parliament over the whole Empire; but nevertheless, this superintendence must be consistent with the fundamental rules of the constitution for "in all free States the Constitution is fixed; and as the supreme Legislative derives its Power and Authority from the Constitution, it cannot overleap the Bounds of it without destroying its own foundation."[26]

My previous discussion has been in vain, unless it appears to my readers entirely natural that the colonists in Massachusetts—taught by their ministers, holding fast to the doctrine that God Himself is a constitutional monarch, and that arbitrary, wilful, and unjust government is illegal government— that these colonists should grasp at a statement made by an eminent writer on law and philosophy, which rang in perfect tune with their own thinking, their own desires, and their own religion.

If we look forward from 1768, when the circular

[25] Vattel, **The Law of Nations,** (fourth ed., London, 1811), II.
[26] Samuel Adams, **Writings,** (H. A. Cushing ed), I, 185.

letter was written, we find the doctrine of the letter and the sentiments of Vattel appearing where we might expect they would appear—in discussions concerning the right of a court to declare a statute to be without legal basis. The first case commonly referred to after the Declaration of Independence was Holmes v. Walton, (1780). Unfortunately the full facts and the nature of the decision are confused or uncertain.[27] In the celebrated case of Trevett v. Weeden (1786) the counsel for Weeden referred to Locke and Vattel and declared that the legislature derived its power from the constitution and had no power of making laws but in subordination of the constitution. In the North Carolina case of 1787 (Bayard and Wife v. Singleton), the court, giving its decision against a legislative act, said that no Act that the legislature could pass "could by any means repeal or alter the constitution, because, if they could do this, they would, at the same instant of time, destroy their own existence as a Legislature, and dissolve the government thereby established."

If we return for a moment to the pronouncements of Massachusetts in 1768, we find, as I said of Otis's speech on the Writs of Assistance, in reality a declaration of Parliament's limited authority; Britons, whether they were on this side of the ocean or the other, were entitled to live under the protection of a fixed and unalterable constitution. Why was it unalterable in essentials? Because it embodied the fundamental principles of unchanging right, reason, and justice. When the colonists claimed the full enjoyment of the fundamental rules of the British constitution they asserted it to be 'an essential, unalterable right, in nature, engrafted into the British constitution, as a fundamental law, and ever held sacred and irrevocable by the subjects within the realm, that what a man has honestly acquired is absolutely his own, which he may freely give, but cannot be taken from him without his consent; that the American subjects may, therefore, exclusive of any con-

[27] Discussed by Austin Scott in **American Hist. Rev.**, IV, 456. Vigorously attacked as a precedent in L. B. Boudin, **Government by Judiciary**, 536 et seq.

sideration of charter rights, with a decent firmness, adapted to the character of free men and subjects, assert this natural and constitutional right."[28] We gain no special comfort by asserting that the colonists had no right either to assign to Britain the possession of a fixed constitution unchangeable by Parliament, or to claim the legally binding character of the law of nature. The important fact is their actually doing so.

In any consideration of the right of a court to declare a statute void, in any attempt to discover how such constitutional principles came to be established, we are carried back to the main line of constitutional argument before actual rebellion. The courts of the states, when they assumed the power to ignore unconstitutional acts, though they were not expressly or by any very evident implication authorized to assume this power, were actually making real the philosophy of the Revolution, which in its turn was based on the old philosophy to which I have given so much attention.

In the many criticisms directed against the courts during the last century and a half, one rarely finds any attack upon the principle that the legislature must not break the constitution. What we do find is the assertion of the legislature's right to be the judge of the extent of its own power. (Those making such assertions, be it noted, never apply this doctrine to the executive or his agents.) There is no space here to examine this argument. But this may be said: If there is any principle which time, the real creator of constitutional principles, establish-

[28] MacDonald, **Select Charters**, 332. Such assertions by eager colonists anxious to find legal ground for objecting to stamp and tariff duties, may seem to the reader extravagant and to be based on the vaguest fabric of a dream; but the learned among them were able to refer to the words of Coke, not only in the Bonham Case, but in Calvin's Case. This latter case Adams knew. Coke said, 1. "That ligeance or obedience of the subject to the Sovereign is due by the law of nature: 2. **That this law of nature is part of the laws of England:** 3. That the law of nature was before any judicial or municipal law in the world: 4. That the law of nature is immutable, and cannot be changed." The emphasis is mine. If Coke here emphasized obedience to the sovereign as a part of natural law, he also emphatically declared that natural law was a part—shall we say?—of the constitution. The above quotation I take from **The Higher Law Background of American Constitutional Law,** an able and learned article by Professor E. S. Corwin in **Harvard Law Review,** XLII, Nos. 2 and 3, p. 369.

ed as essentially American doctrine, it is the doctrine that no man is bound by anything but the law. Would that we could live up to its practice, and not fall victim so often to the bandit and the racketeer! The courts without direct written and explicit mandate from the people gave to that doctrine such force and sanction as their judicial independence enabled them to give.

Before leaving this subject which I have attempted to work out from the time of Robert Browne, I wish to say just a word about colonists outside of New England. They too, when the argument against Parliament began, insisted upon the legal right of America and the illegal conduct of Parliament. But if we examine the writings of the leading and more influential statesmen of the middle and southern colonies, we find the social-compact idea much less prominent than in New England. For instance, John Dickinson of Pennsylvania, whose writings were very influential, could find principles in the make-up of the Empire, as a working system, and in the legal structure of the mother country, without enlarging upon "the laws of nature and of nature's God"; and he found opportunity to remind Englishmen that their rights had in part been won by rebellion.[29]

In Dickinson's arguments we find the unquestionable influence of his legal training and the atmosphere in which he had studied the elements of his profession. He had studied law in the English Inns of Court. He and the others of like training did not come forward as ignorant novices, uninitiated into the mysteries of English law; nor did they gather their arguments so much from the philosophy of the Rebellion of the mid-seventeenth century, as from long history of English liberty. It is interesting to think of these young colonists, from the middle and southern colonies, foregathering with their fellow British students about the hospitable board of the Middle or Inner Temple. There they discussed, we may well assume, the principles of English law and doubtless also

[29] Yet Dickinson himself at a later day gave a not uncertain recognition to the compact-theory. See **The Federalist and Other Constitutional Papers**, (E. H. Scott ed.), 789.

the nature and the obligations of the British imperial system and the rights of the colonists; and they had full opportunity to do this in the days before the acute question of Parliamentary authority had reached the stage of bitter contention. Arguments in favor of American rights were not, presumably, new and untried weapons in their hands when the Stamp Act and the Revenue Act were passed and American indignation was aroused. These men had not sat in the uncomfortable pews of a New England meeting-house and listened to preachers disclosing the secrets of the scriptures; as students of law they battled and argued (I am allowing myself the assumption) with their fellows amid the solemn inspiring shadows of the Elizabethan hall of the old Middle Temple. We well assume that this training enabled Dickinson to present a picture of the Empire as a consistent whole, in which the rights of the colonies were constitutionally protected, and probably it led him to accept only with reluctance and hesitation the necessity of announcing independence and of protecting with arms the rights of the colonists on the principle of English liberty. And still no one more succinctly than Dickinson, in his famous *Letters from a Pennsylvania Farmer,*[30] pronounced the doctrine of limited government; and, when all is said, that was the center of the colonial position: "For who are a free people? Not those, over whom government is reasonably and equitably exercised, but those who live under a government so constitutionally checked and controlled, that proper provision is made against its being otherwise exercised." To lose sight of this rumor of war, or to be content with visions of broken tea-boxes and even embattled farmers, is to miss the pivotal fact. The colonists were demanding a constitutionally checked government; they claimed it was already theirs; and in course of time they proceeded not only to fight, but to create governments of exactly that character.

The signal statement made by the Pennsylvania Farmer probably seems to you an inadequate defi-

---

[30] **The Letters** were widely circulated. A modern reprint is in **Memoirs of the Historical Society of Pennsylvania,** Vol. XIV.

nition of a free people. One may well question whether one has real liberty solely because of the existence of a constitutionally limited government. So greatly has the world changed in the last century and a half; so complicated has modern society become because of the invention of machinery and the increase of population; so interrelated are men of one community or of one nation with the interests and activities of others, that a government strictly checked lest it interfere with individual rights does not appear to be the consummation of political wisdom. A government hampered in its activities, checked by courts, which are themselves, in considerable measure, controlled and checked by the principles of the eighteenth century—a government which is unable to reach out and correct at will social abuses or economic evils, is not of the kind, we are told, which can assure real liberty for the masses of men or register and promote any substantial progress. It is not my intention to combat such modern notions or to applaud them, but only to impress upon your minds the long historical process which brought into actual institutional form and practice the principles that there are individual rights which no government can rightfully ignore and that free government is government constitutionally checked.

No one can say to what extent these historical antecedents were actually and patently causative— to what extent men were consciously carrying out a long historical process and were conscious that they were embodying in their institutions the teachings of the past. But of interest to us is the continuity of a tendency and the permanence or semi-permanence of an idea. It need not disturb us very much to discover that the forces of history were working silently and carrying their products along on the currents of time, even though men were not fully aware of the processes at work. By such courses and apparently uncharted channels, time and human effort and human desire move along toward their goal. But some of the American leaders were men of erudition; some of them knew their "wisest writers"; some of them had conned philosophy and history; all of them had experience in life and politics.

VI

The Foundations of Federalism

IN THE PRECEDING pages I have been dealing with certain essential principles which have been established in our institutions, and I have paid particular attention to the history of New England. No attention has been paid to what you may think to be the most important of all—the nature of the federal state as distinguished from the unitary state. To that subject it seems appropriate to give a few moments of consideration. Time does not permit extensive comment, and I propose to present only a few prominent facts.

The fully organized and articulated federal state is a form of political order of the first importance. Its creation in America constitutes a signal contribution to political theory and practice. A federal state is a political system, wherein substantial powers of sovereignty within the body-politic are not confined to a single government but distributed among governments. It is most easily described as a system in which sovereignty is divided, and such was the conception commonly held by the men who established the system a hundred and forty-five years ago. But since the doctrine of divided sovereignty is now discredited as a principle of political science, and since the common definition of sovereignty—absolute and complete authority—banishes the possibility of division (for how can you divide and limit and set bounds upon the absolute and the complete?), it may seem best to speak of the federal state, not as one characterized by the distribution of sovereignty itself, but characterized by the distribution of sovereign powers. This latter definition leaves something to be desired. But we may content ourselves with saying that a federal state is a body made up of states; the various members are more than administrative districts; they have a very considerable degree of irresponsible autonomy.[1] So long as the federal state exists as a federal state, the constituent members are legally entitled to manage that portion of their affairs which the law consigns to them, or, in the American system, leaves to them. This distribution is supposed to have a large degree of permanence. Ruthless and wanton interference or such substantial alteration as actually destroys the authority and greatly reduces the scope of power in the commonwealths is contrary to the theory of federalism, and if carried to its ultimate, of course destroys federalism itself.

Considerable attention has been paid in textbooks and in other histories to various schemes and plans of union in colonial times. These are significant, because they indicate a real though faint recognition of the need of union. But it cannot be said that they had any very noticeable effect. It is worth while to notice the processes by which the men of Rhode Island succeeded in the seventeenth century in making a substantial merger of settlements. The New England Confederation, which lasted for some fifty years, probably had influence on the later plans for organizing the American Union.

Special attention, however, should be paid to the Albany Plan of Union of 1754, which was largely Franklin's handiwork. It was probably influential at a later time, and is very significant because it so clearly points to the necessity of granting certain power to a grand colonial council, and, in the selection of those powers, it anticipated in some measure

---

[1] The difficulty of exact definition arises from the fact that, in every government, powers are actually distributed, or may be so spoken of. Furthermore, in the United States, there is one supreme sovereignty, if I may be allowed the expression, viz., the authority which can amend the Constitution; and by such action it may take away sovereign powers from the localities and present them to the central government, and can, legally speaking, alter in almost any conceivable way the assignment of authority. My contention is only this: as long as the essentials of federalism exist, the whole system must continue to present conditions in which the commonwealths have many of the powers and responsibilities of actually autonomous bodies.

the work of the men at Philadelphia in 1787. Anything and everything that gave evidence of a comprehension of the need of singling out certain powers as of general rather than local importance, any word or plan that appears to us to indicate a grasp of the problem of distribution and the creation of a composite system, is of importance to the student of American history. By the middle of the eighteenth century, in the presence of the French menace and the Indian peril, the need for coöperation and union was plainly evident. But on what terms? "Every Body," said Franklin, disappointed by the cold reception of the Albany Plan, "cries, a Union is absolutely necessary; but when they come to the Manner and Form of the Union, their weak Noddles are perfectly distracted."[2]

The difficulty, then, was the manner and form of union, rather than the desirability of union. It need not surprise us that this was the case. The problem was complex. To solve it, a way must be found which would give expression to the fact of diversification, as well as to the fact of unity and the need of coöperation. The task required not distracted noddles, but the best minds which statesmen had at their command. As events proved, it took a generation of trial and error, the breaking of the Empire, painful and disheartening experience, to bring about the establishment of the Union, which recognized in its form and manner the integral character of each commonwealth and the essential integrity of the whole. Until the Revolutionary War broke out, this task of imperial order confronted British statesmen rather more than American. By the end of the old French war (1763), the time had clearly come when there needed to be a distinct understanding of the respective fields of government which would be occupied by the home authorities on the one hand and by the colonies on the other. After war began and independence was decided upon by the colonies, the task of imperial organization passed into the hands of the American statesmen.

[2] **Writings of Franklin**, (A. H. Smyth ed.), III, 242.

Franklin's scheme, as it appears in the Albany Plan, was a scheme for solving the problem of the British Empire; it was produced by the experiences and the perplexities of that Empire. It was not a plan for the assumption of colonial power antagonistic to the mother country, nor was it a plan for obtaining independence. It must primarily take its place in the history of the British imperial system. It reminds us that the great problem of that generation of Britons was the problem of imperial organization, finding a method whereby the continuity and the effectiveness of the Empire could be assured. The task was there, but British statesmen did not grasp the essentials. Most of them saw it only in its crudest form. They saw only the desirability of centralized authority, to be exercised freely and largely in disregard of the actual character of the Empire.

But the imperial system could not flourish in disregard of historical fact, and the main fact was the existence of colonial governments, some of which had been active and competent for over a hundred years. Nothing can be more absurd than to suppose that Massachusetts, Virginia, or Connecticut would or could submit to treatment which by implication indicated their inability to manage their own affairs within a limited field, and especially to be free from taxation imposed upon them by the government at Westminster.

We have seen the Americans insisting strongly upon individual right, upon the necessity of limited government, for only under limited government could personal liberty be safe. The main theme of this lecture is the creation of a system of union which recognized the liberty of states under law. When the days of argument against Parliamentary power began, the men of America insisted upon colonial competence. When Parliament passed the Sugar Act of 1764 and the Stamp Act a year later, the Americans demanded the recognition of the rights of the colonies, as bodies corporate, constituent members of the Empire. Two ideas, therefore, not one, are conspicious—individual liberty and (very clearly at first) local liberty within the British Empire. These demands were mutually supporting: individual liberty and the principle of a divided or composite empire in which each of the colonies would have its share of constitutional authority, an authority which should be recognized in the law of the empire.

We thus find again the Americans claiming as already existing what in reality they were about to create. And still, this is not wholly true. As a matter of plain fact, the colonies, as I have already pointed out, had been largely in control of their own affairs; and the Empire as a practical working system was characterized by diversificaton and not by centralization. But, with the Stamp Act, there arose the demand on both sides of the ocean for the settlement of constitutional principles. The Englishmen—most of them—insisted that, by constitutional and legal right, Parliament had supreme power and the duty of the colonists was to obey; by the law of the Empire, unlimited authority was in the Parliament. The colonists pointed to their own liberties, both individual and corporate, and insisted upon legal recognition of the privileges and authority to which they had been accustomed. When I say, then, that the colonists were claiming as their own what in reality they were going to create, the statement means this: they declared the British Empire, as thus existing, was a composite empire, within which as a matter of law each colony had a definite measure of independent authority. They thus proclaimed as already existing not so much new rights as distinct constitutional acknowledgment of those rights as *legally* their own; and they demanded the kind of empire which in considerable degree had already existed as a practical fact; but they were to create in the course of that generation an empire of their own—the United States—which gave full legal expression of unity, central authority, and that diversification which is the heart of federalism.

The colonists insisted particularly upon their right to be free from Parliamentary taxation; and they based this claim on the constitutional principle which they found embodied in English insular law. They declared in essence that those principles must obtain in the Empire. They thus insisted that English constitutionalism in this particular was the law of the Empire. But they went farther: they claimed the right to manage their own internal affairs without undue interference by the hand of government at Westminster. And the task of making clear the extent of local as distinguished from imperial authority was performed with difficulty. Had there not been the actual teachings of practical experience, this job would have been impossible to accomplish. It may seem to you a strange, even an unpatriotic statement, to say that the American federal state was the child of the old British Empire, because the Americans gave legal and institutional reality to the principle of diversification of powers and thus crystallized a system much like that under which the colonists had grown to maturity.

This argumentative contest in which the Americans set up the rights of the colonists as corporate entities in the Empire is illustrated by Patrick Henry's famous Stamp Act resolutions passed by the Virginia House: *"Resolved,* That the taxation of the people by themselves or by persons chosen by themselves to represent them, who can only know what taxes the people are able to bear, and the easiest mode of raising them, and are equally affected by such taxes themselves, is the distinguishing characteristic of British freedom, and without which the ancient constitution cannot subsist."[3] Here, therefore, we find a declaration of individual liberty, protected by the principles of the British constitution, and the liberty specially mentioned is that of taxing themselves through their own representatives. But Henry's proposals also point clearly to the traditional and the legal right of Virginia not only to levy taxes but also to manage its own internal affairs: *"Resolved,* That his majesty's liege people of this most

[3] This resolution does not appear to have been one of those distributed among the colonies, but in the set passed by the House. Cf. M. C. Tyler, **Patrick Henry,** 70-74.

ancient colony have uninterruptedly enjoyed the right of being thus governed by their own assembly in the article of their taxes and internal police, and that the same hath never been forfeited, or any other way given up, but hath been constantly recognized by the kings and people of Great Britain."

At first, and indeed to the end, the degree of power which should be considered to be within the field of the colonies, was not definitely and precisely outlined by the various American arguments. The Stamp Act Congress of 1765 alleging the right of the colonies to be free from Parliamentary taxation acknowledged "all due subordination to that august body the parliament of Great Britain." And in Massachusetts we find the town of Boston insisting that the power granted by royal charter "of making laws for our internal Government and of levying Taxes" was vested in the colonial legislature. Though the difficulty of drawing the line between imperial power and colonial autonomy was inevitable, this may be said: to the last, or certainly almost to the time of declared independence, the colonists would apparently have been content with the old traditional system under which they had lived; and that system in very large measure left to the colonies their right to manage their own internal affairs, a right that was occasionally, and more or less effectively, controlled in particular instances by the Crown rather than by Parliament. There was, it is true, some legislation which immediately or remotely affected the colonies.

But at a fairly early time in the argumentative conflict some men grasped the idea, though not fully; they saw the need of distinguishing between one governmental power and another. And this deserves special attention, because only on the basis of distinction between powers can the kind of political system known to you and me stand. Otis and Dulany, for example, in exceedingly able pamphlets, indicated the difference between taxation and the regulation of trade, or, as we now say, the difference between taxation and regulation of commerce. This distinction was in reality based upon the prac-

tice of the Empire; for the Parliament had not levi-
ed taxes internally upon the colonies; and though
some of the navigation acts had incidentally or on
their face appeared to be acts for revenue, their
purpose was to direct the course of trade. Any distinction, whether you think it a good one or not,
which deals with the idea that distinctions can be
made, is important to the student of constitutional
history, if he is desirous of seeing the sources from
which there came the essential quality of the American constitutional system.

Now, in this connection we should clearly see, as
I have already said, that here is just where English
statesmanship failed or, rather, where statesmanship
did not appear at all. It is true that some men of
superior wisdom manfully proclaimed in Parliament
the inherent right of the colonists. Lord Camden, for
example, eloquently denounced Parliamentary taxation, as did Pitt. Burke, with magnificent statesmanship, deplored the lack of practical wisdom and
declared that large empires and small minds went ill
together. Characteristically, however, Burke did not
dwell upon constitutional rights in any narrow and
technical sense. He said he wished to be guided not
by what a lawyer told him he had the power to do,
but by what his own sense of right and justice told
him he ought to do. There is no nobler expression
in the course of the Revolutionary discussion. Empires must flourish, if they flourish at all, on justice,
not merely on naked legal power. But the times
called or seemed to call, for legal determinations of
legal rights and for legal limitations of power. And
the die hards in Britain, more distinctly I think at the
beginning than a little later when their tempers were
somewhat cooled, made their position perfectly manifest: powers could not be distinguished one from
the other; Parliament had either all powers or none;
deny to Parliament the possession of complete power
and you necessarily deny that it has any.

Among the Americans the person making the
most valuable contribution to the idea that powers
could be distinguished one from the other was John
Dickinson. In his Farmer's Letters he attacked the

distinction, which was more or less commonly spoken of, between internal and external taxation. A tax, he declared, was an imposition for raising revenue; no matter where the burden fell, whether within the colony or at the customs office, a tax was a tax. Regulation of intercolonial and foreign commerce, however, was a natural and inevitable power of empire. He acknowledged that Parliament, as the superintending authority in the Empire, was and should be possessed of that power. The distinction was real; it was consistent with the actual practice of the Empire; or, at the very least, the basis of the distinction was apparent in what had been done and what had not been done; it is found within our own constitutional sytem.

In the resolutions passed by the Continental Congress in 1774, the colonists passed far beyond the position of claiming the possession of individual liberty or of asserting, with some apparent misgivings or at least without full precision, just what the rights of the colonists as such were. Impelled in part by the British persistence in claiming complete authority for Parliament, and helped along by Governor Hutchinson's declaration in Massachusetts that there could not be two independent legislatures in one and the same state, the more advanced American leaders had come to the point where they denied that Parliament had the right to govern them in any respect whatever; and that appears to be the position definitely announced in the Declaration and Resolves of 1774. And yet Congress proclaimed the willingness of the colonists to consent to Parliamentary acts for the regulation of external commerce. This consent, it was said, arose "from the necessity of the case." Thus they asserted the possibility of distinguishing between one power and others; and they acknowledged the need, in the interest of both the colonies and the mother country, of one central authority to regulate commerce.

One of the central questions of the Revolution was, therefore, whether federalism was possible as a theory of political organization—freedom at least in the sense of distributed authority. By asserting the impossibility, Britain lost her empire, lost it because of obedience to a theory of law and political power, lost it because, influenced still by insularism, she could not see in reality, in practice, in the actual workings of the Empire during several generations, there had been an Empire in which powers were parcelled out among governments. She refused to acknowledge as the law of the Empire the facts which her liberal and free-handed policy had created. The Britons insisted on a legal theory, and the Americans were scarcely less legalistic; both sides desired to see the question of legal right settled. The Americans succeeded five years after the war ended in establishing an empire of law, setting up a constitution of empire which declared itself to be an empire marked by the distribution rather than by the concentration of authority.

Repetition may not be unwise. The principles of federalism were in reality embodied in the *practice* of the old Empire; that is to say, the most simple and elementary fact is the most important: the Empire in practice was not a thoroughly consolidated and centralized Empire. Colonies did exist, and had long existed, in possession of governments of their own with many powers and with actual authority. Furthermore, the more conspicious powers which had been exercised by the Home Government were those powers naturally belonging there from *the necessity of the case,* powers that could not well be exercised by the colonies—the post-office, naturalization, war and peace, foreign affairs, intercolonial and foreign commerce, establishment of new colonies, etc.—in other words, the powers which are the chief powers assigned to the central government in our own federal system. So again we find America after the Revolution, while making a great contribution to the political system of the world, actually building upon the past, institutionalizing practices, establishing an empire of law, creating constitutional federalism.

It is an important fact that the Revolution must be considered as a contest for the recognition of local rights as well as individual rights. Modern days have seen, and the present day is seeing, much discussion concerning the rights of the states of the American Union; and the question sometimes arises whether the Union is or can long be looked upon as a federal union, within which the central government has only the power granted and is supposed to be entrusted only with duties of a national as distinguished from a local character. Once more I have no desire to express dogmatic judgments. Human institutions cannot stand still. Nationalism is the product of the railroad, the telegraph, the telephone, and all other instruments by which men are held together or merged into a common mass; and a political system must accommodate and adjust itself to actual social and economic condition; it cannot successfully fight the stars in their courses or refute by legal argument the results of the discoveries of the scientist in his laboratory. It is, however, well to notice that the Revolutionary movement included within itself zeal for colonial privileges as well as for personal liberties.

The Americans, then, were announcing, though at times only vaguely, the principle of federalism[4]— a system of political order in which powers are distributed among governments. Such a system is scarcely workable unless it be founded upon law and bound by law. For each government must keep within the field marked out for it and must not force its way into the field of another. Local rights of the separate commonwealths must be made clear and maintained by distinct formulation of plain law. And so we find here the blending of this idea of law as the basis of federalism with the conception of the reign of law in the civil state—a conception which we have seen set forth in the centuries long gone by as a protection to the individual citizen. Without its application to a composite empire, that empire could

[4] More plainly in some respects before 1773 or 1774. At that late date, the leaders began, as we have seen, openly, and some of them, like John Adams, with great legal acumen, to contend that Parliament had no authority at all. And we should notice again in this connection that the Declaration of Independence did not announce independence from Parliament, but rather the overthrow of the king, who had unkinged himself by giving his consent to "acts of pretended legislation." There was no need, according to this line of approach, to declare independence of Parliament, inasmuch as no obedience had been due.

be only temporary, or it would be subject to spasmo-dic change or fall victim to uproar and tumult. The two great achievements of the Revolutionary epoch —which I have thus shown were indeed interrelated and interdependent—were (1) the establishment of governments limited by law and under obligation to protect individual liberty, and (2) the establishment in 1788 of a federal system based on law.

We must now pass on to a consideration of the at-tempts of the Americans to set up their imperial system, to find for themselves a solution to the prob-lem of imperial organization.

The first attempt to organize a general continental system was not completely successful. The Articles of Confederation, which went forth from Congress in 1777 and were adopted by the last state in 1781, were by no means a failure, however; both the merits and the faults of the scheme pointed the way to success. The plan of distribution of power, though not altogether suited to actual needs, on the whole approached perfection. And that was so because the scheme was in considerable degree based on colonial experience and on the system of the old Empire. The Articles marked out with considerable precision the power that should belong to a national govern-ment; and in this respect they were of immense ser-vice to the framers of the Constitution ten years later. Of special consequence too is their provision for a court of judicature with the right to settle disputes between states. This authority and this power of judicial determination provided for by the Articles passed into the Constitution of the United States. We have a right to pride ourselves on the authority of the Supreme Court to pass upon controversies of that kind. If the Union, as the Articles stated on their face, was only a league of sovereignties, this pro-vision for judicial settlement by an international tribunal (an intersovereign court) is to-day of pe-culiar interest. It pointed unerringly to the fact that, if states setting themselves up as sovereign hoped to live in peace and amity, controversies must be settled by a tribunal in accord with the principles and obligations of law. Attention should be paid also to the provisions in the Articles for the recognition of interstate comity; for those provisions were with slight modification embodied in the Constitution, and thus stand to-day as constitutional obligations binding the quasi-sovereign states of the Union.

The federal Convention met at Philadelphia in May, 1787. It was called ". . . for the sole and express purpose of revising the Articles of Confederation, and reporting to Congress and the several Legislatures, such alterations and provisions therein, as shall . . . render the federal Constitution adequate to the exigencies of Government, and the preservation of the Union."[5] In reality the country had no constitution, properly speaking; and the Union, such as it was, appeared to be on the verge of complete collapse. The job of the Convention, which called for the highest and broadest statesmanship and wisdom, was to solve the problem of imperial organization, to provide a system which should live and work, which should recognize and properly guard the individual rights and the powers of the states, and which should nevertheless weave the states and their people into a permanent union.

Among the noteworthy qualities of this body of able men, we find two which now appear preëminent. The first is the reign of patience almost altogether untarnished by petulant declamation. Though there is evidence of intense earnestness, and though there was some heartburning, when a decision was reached contrary to the desire of one group or another, the disappointed delegates did not resort to sulky altercation; there was, in general, a spirit of coöperation and a readiness to accommodate and compose differences. The Constitution is sometimes called a bundle of compromises; it may be more justly called the product of adjustment. The second noteworthy fact is the practical character of the Convention's proceedings. There was, it is true, considerable presentation of political theory. Some of it seems old-fashioned to-day, and some of it even then was not highly appropriate. But there was little of the vapor-

[5] **Documentary History of the Constitution,** I, 8, Feb. 21, 1787.

ing of revolutionaries or that tendency, which we think of as characteristic of the late eighteenth century, to deal with disembodied ideas. Although the philosophy of Tom Paine, who had declared that the palaces of kings were built on the ruins of the bowers of paradise, had gained some footing in America, we nevertheless find in the Convention no desire to pull down all human governmental contrivances, to return by one leap to the age of primeval bliss and to ignore the teachings of history and the lessons of actual experience.

Before taking up one or two cardinal problems which the Convention faced and solved, it may be well in this year of celebration and thankfulness to say a word about George Washington, who was chosen president of that body. There is, or was, an inclination in this country to relegate him to a position which in some respects is little above mediocrity; he was, we are sometimes told, a patient, plodding man, possessed of sterling virtue but without the incisive qualities of the political artists, and without the powers of creative statesmanship. To insist that Washington had such learning in law, or history, or political theory, as James Wilson or Madison had, would be absurd. But he did have a peculiar quality, the ability to hit in a few words at the very heart of a difficulty, to grasp essentials unerringly. Not long before the Convention met, Washington said, "I do not conceive we can exist long as a nation without having lodged somewhere a power, which will pervade the whole Union in as energetic a manner as the authority of the State governments extends over the several States." You can read many pages of historical narrative or of political disquisition without finding anything which presents, so adequately the problems of 1787 and the pivotal principle upon which an answer depended.

As president of the Convention, Washington had little opportunity to speak. But many of the questions were debated in the committee of the whole, when he was not in the chair. He spoke only once, and then on a matter which was important but probably not critical. Madison, who in some respects was particularly well-prepared, spoke often and ably, and Washington apparently relied on Madison's power of thoughtful analysis and judicious discussion. And still the Convention's respect for Washington's partriotism, wisdom, and big-mindedness was effective; perhaps it may be said of him at that time, as Monroe said after the Constitution had been adopted by Virginia, that the influence of George Washington caused the acceptance of the Constitution. I do not know anything more futile than the motion that statesmanship is evidenced by fluent oratory, or even by incisive logic, and that wisdom, supreme good sense, self-control, faculty for thinking plainly, seeing clearly, and acting judiciously, are not the essential ingredients of successful public service and superb achievement.

Of the work of the Convention and the way in which it met the most difficult problems, time allows only a few words. I will confine myself to a brief discussion of certain salient measures which illustrate the solution of the problem of imperial order. The most prominent thing is of course the full exposition of the principle and doctrine of federalism, the establishment of the federal state, that system of political order which reconciles local liberty with national or imperial unity.

The main trouble during the period of the Confederation was the unwillingness of the states to abide by their obligations. The Articles purported to be the basis of "perpetual union"; but there could be no perpetuity or semblance of order if the states either wilfully or negligently went their way without respect for the powers granted to the Congress and without regard for the rights of their neighbors or their own duties as constituent members of the whole system. Under any scheme of union, what assurance could there be of permanence, if the states continued to act in disregard of their obligations? When the Convention met, therefore, the central question was plainly how to create a system whereby there would be just this assurance; some plan must be found which would make fairly certain a workable, continuing union. It is probably not necessary that I should emphasize this fact; the Confederation was near complete ruin, it was an acknowledged failure, because the states disregarded their duties as members of the Union. No union could last unless it were so organized that there would be reasonable assurance that the states would play their part. How to answer that pressing problem confronted the Convention at the very outset of its labours.

So strongly was this thought held by the most determined unionists, that the first general scheme for the new system, which was presented by Randolph in behalf of the Virginia delegates, proposed the establishment of a national government. It was properly so called and was properly distinguished from a congress in a confederation of sovereignties. Furthermore, to meet the question, which I have called the main question of the time, this Virginia plan contained three explicit answers: (1) that state officers should be bound by oath to support the Articles of Union; (2) that the national legislature should be empowered to veto all laws passed by states contravening in the opinion of the national legislature the Articles of Union; (3) that the legislature (i.e., Congress) should be empowered "to call forth the force of the Union against any member of the Union failing to fulfil its duty under the Articles thereof."[6]

Of these three proposals, only one, the first, went into the Constitution as a finished document. Why were the other two dropped? The right and the power to coerce a delinquent state—to use war against the state as a corporate body—was seen, as the work of the Convention went on, to be inconsistent with the very theory or principle of nationalism. Governments enforce law upon their citizens; war is the old time-worn and barbaric method used by one nation against another. The Constitution and the law should rest on people; governmental acts should be directed to individual citizens. James Wilson spoke of "the twofold relation in which the people would stand,—first, as citizens of the General

[6] May 29, 1787.

Government; and secondly as citizens of their particular State. . . . With respect to the province and object of the General Government they [the state governments] should be considered as having no existence."[7] Thus, coercion of states as such was abandoned for the acceptance of a national system; the principle accepted was characteristic of American federalism. Governments are to be kept as distinctly as possible within their respective fields, and neither is to be, in ordinary operation, in contact with the other. We often in these latter days think of the government at Washington as a government over the states and superior to them. But such is not our constitutional system. There is in our federal system no superiority or inferiority; the state and the nation (acting through the government) each has its share of political authority; each government operates, supposedly absolutely without friction and without the clash resulting from governmental jealousy, directly upon its own citizens. The Constitution when framed recognized the principle that Hamilton later announced—the principle that a government over governments is a solecism in politics. It has no place in the American scheme of things. I doubt if there is anything more needful for an understanding of the American federal state than a realization of this simple fact, that the national government and the state governments are each supreme within their respective fields.

The proposal to give Congress the power to veto state laws was also abandoned. It was more strongly defended than the proposal for coercion, but proved unacceptable. The exercise of such a power we can plainly see would have affronted state pride and almost surely awakened resentment. It was similar to the old disallowance of colonial acts by the king in council. Madison, indeed, when advocating the adoption of the negative, referred to this old royal practice. It had been not ineffective in the old Empire; but it did not conduce to good feeling and harmony. The anxiety felt by some of the strongest

[7] June 25.

advocates of an efficient government and a permanent union is strikingly illustrated by Madison's insistence for considerable time on the necessity of granting this right to negative state laws; Charles Pinckney continued his advocacy almost to the end. A power of negativing improper state laws, Madison said, "is at once the most mild and certain means of preserving the harmony of the system."[8]

The discussion of this subject is of extreme importance for any one wishing to understand the greatest difficulty of the time and the nature of the Union as the Convention gradually worked out its essential principle. After Madison's speech, Gouverneur Morris declared, "A law that ought to be negatived [meaning of course a state law], will be set aside in the Judiciary department; and if that security should fail, may be repealed by a National law." Roger Sherman then made a most significant statement: "Such a power [the negative upon state acts] involves a wrong principle, to wit, that a law of a State contrary to the Articles of the Union would, if not negativated, be valid and operative."[9] The Convention thereupon voted against giving this power to the national legislature, and Luther Martin of Maryland immediately offered a resolution, which was adopted. In somewhat modified form that resolution appears in the Constitution in the following words: "This Constitution, and the laws of the United States which shall be made in pursuance thereof; and all Treaties made, or which shall be made, under the authority of the United States, shall be the supreme law of the land; and the judges in every State shall be bound thereby; anything in the Constitution or laws of any State to the Contrary notwithstanding." The Constitution was made law, enforceable in courts.

Is it necessary to comment on the interesting significance of this pronouncement? It contains the principle to which so much attention has been given in these lectures. That principle is made the keystone of the new system. Any legislative act beyond the

8 July 17, 1787.
9 July 17.

competence of a legislative body is not law. The principle is by compelling logic applicable to Congress; and if we accept this logic, no act passed by Congress contrary to the Constitution is law;[10] and furthermore courts are under compulsion to disregard an act of such a character. But we should notice carefully: the chief purpose in the minds of the framers of the Constitution was to put obligation on the *states* and the *state* judiciary to respect the laws and the Constitution of the United States. The reign of law, the fundamental principle which we have seen to be a part of the old compact-philosophy and of Puritan theology—the principle which was the basis of Revolutionary argument against Parliament—was now made the essential principle of federalism. The states were to be held together, the Union was to be conserved, and essential harmony of the system was to be maintained, not by a new doctrine, but by the old. The courts of the states and (it would seem as a logical sequence) the courts of the Union are bound by law not to give their assent to "acts of pretended legislation"—those words which appear in the Declaration of Independence as the groundwork of the charges against George III.

In the Constitution of the United States, therefore, we find this principle of limited government bound by law reaching its ultimate. The concept was of hoary antiquity, but it had not been properly and fully institutionalized. I mean by this, of course, that the idea that governments, if they act lawfully, must respect natural rights and natural justice, and must be bound and limited by the law of nature, was a very old idea; but the Americans in framing the

[10] There has been discussion as to whether the Convention intended to provide for judicial power to set aside Congressional acts, or expected that such power would be used. See Charles Beard, **The Supreme Court and the Constitution.** L. B. Boudin, **Government by Judiciary,** strongly attacks the so-called precedents. But if the precedents had no existence how are we to account for Gerry's saying in the Convention (June 4) "In some States the judges had actually set aside laws, as being against the constitution." The principle seems to have been well known by the members and was referred to. Cf. Martin's statement, July 21st. There was not unanimity on the desirability of the power. It seems at least probable that the members, who were not lacking in astuteness, must have comprehended the effect of explicitly announcing that the Constitution was law.

Constitution used the principle of limited government as the central and controlling principle of the
federal state. In making it the central and pivotal
principle on which the working system of a federal
state (a composite empire) should stand, the founders of the Constitution gave it an exalted position.
In his demand for a "standing law to live by," Locke
could see no farther than the right to rebel against
an act transcending the authority of the legislature,
which was in theory bound by the law of nature, a
law to all men. As in other matters the Americans
had succeeded in giving concrete formulation of
doctrines, so in this case they did more than repeat
phrases; they made the Constitution law in the fullest
sense of the word; they called upon courts to recognize the principle that an act beyond law is no law,
and, as I have said, used it as the basis for maintaining the permanence of the Union in a wide-
flung empire. The right of revolution was, so to
speak, domesticated, the right to oppose unconstitutional law; but if the theory of the Constitution
was lived up to, there was no need of war and tumult to protect law; "no appeal to heaven" would be
necessary, but an appeal to courts; so far as human
ingenuity could solve the problem through institutions and practices, forceful revolution was made
unnecessary by the injunction upon the courts to
recognize and apply the fundamental law. Not to
the masses of men in rebellion was the right assigned
or conceded of opposing governmental violation of
law, but to the individual litigant appearing in a
court of justice.

It will be noticed, I have not spent much time in
discussing that task of the federal Convention, which
might properly be considered of primal importance
in working out a system of federalism. That system, we have seen, contains as a main characteristic
the distribution of powers among governments. As a
matter of fact, the Convention spent little time upon
that problem. Some difficulty arose concerning the
old question inherited from the earlier days, the
question of bestowing on the central government
the power to regulate interstate and foreign com-

merce. Parliament had exercised that power in colonial times. Because the Congress of the Confederation had not that power in its full possession, there was trouble and confusion. The federal Convention had been called partly to find a remedy for that very difficulty. But the differences between the carrying or commercial states and the staple-raising states threw some doubt upon the propriety of granting to Congress the complete authority over the subject of interstate and foreign commerce, but such authority with slight modification was finally granted. This fact is not for us now a matter of primary importance. The Convention did not need to work out a new and elaborate system of distribution between state and nation, for they were guided by the practices of the old Empire and by the provisions of the Articles of Confederation. The general scheme of distribution of powers lay at their very door; it was within the field of their own experience.

But if federalism was to be set up in the new system, distribution there must be. It is a very interesting fact that the nationalists in the Convention were so determined in the early weeks to establish a national government with real authority and effectiveness, so anxious were they to overcome the disintegrating forces threatening the permanence of union, that they paid little attention to the question of distribution and to the necessity of assuring, not only the authority of the national government, but also the permanence and the autonomy of the states. Federalism requires by its very nature not only central authority, but also local autonomy within a limited field.

No more difficult question ever presented itself to a body of lawmakers. We find in it the very center of the problem of discovering federalism and making it into a workable scheme of government. Had conditions permitted, it might have been a not extraordinarily difficult task to work out the elementary features of a national government possessed of *full* political authority. On the other hand to set up a system of independent states in an elaborate confederation offered no novel and insuperable difficulty. But to strike the balance; to create an effective and permanent union and a powerful government and still maintain the states in the possession of a considerable degree of autonomy, was a task that might well have overtaxed the capacity of the wisest statesmanship. One reason for the difficulty was that the Americans, though taught by experiences in the old Empire and by trial and error, were engaged in the production of a new form of political order. Some delegates eagerly desiring full realization of nationalism were not fully conscious of the problem and not fully alive to the necessities of the case. That is why Hamilton[11] cannot be listed among the Convention leaders; he was so strong a nationalist that he did not adequately envisage federalism—distribution rather than concentration, security for the states as well as authority and power for the national government.

The fact, as I have stated, is that the nationalists in their anxiety for national power were forging ahead so rapidly and victoriously for a time that some members of the Convention began to fear lest the states be totally submerged or at least be gradually swept entirely within the grasp of the central government. The issue was clearly stated by Johnson of Connecticut, one of a trio of able men from that state who were not opposed to an effective government but were determined to preserve the states. On June 21, while the question of whether there should be two branches or one in the national legislature was under consideration, Johnson compared the so-called New Jersey or small-state plan and the Virginia or large-state plan; the latter was nationalistic in scope and purpose. "One gentleman alone (Colonel Hamilton)," said Johnson, ". . . boldly and decisively contended for an abolition of the State Governments. Mr. Wilson and the gentleman from

[11] Hamilton was absent a considerable portion of the time. He was one of three delegates from New York, two of whom were opposed to nationalism and the main trend of the Convention's work. After they left he was unable to cast the vote of his state. His superb defense of the Constitution when it was submitted to the states for adoption has led to the belief that in the Convention itself he was one of the highly constructive leaders.

Virginia . . . held a different language. They wished
to leave the States in possession of a considerable,
though a subordinate, jurisdiction. They had not yet,
however, shewn how this could consist with, or be
secured against, the general sovereignty and jurisdiction which they proposed to give to the National
Government. If this could be shewn, in such a manner as to satisfy the patrons of the New Jersey propo-
sitions, that the individuality of the States would
not be endangered, many of their objections would
no doubt be removed. If this could not be shewn,
their objections would have their full force."

A week later, Johnson made a similar statement:
"The controversy must be endless whilst gentlemen
differ in the grounds of their arguments; those on
one side considering the States as districts of people
composing one political society: those on the other,
considering them as so many political societies. The
fact is, that the States do exist as political societies,
and a government is to be formed for them in their
political capacity, as well as for the individuals composing them. Does it not seem to follow, that if the
States, as such, are to exist, they must be armed
with some power of self-defence?" . . . On the whole
he thought, that, "as in some respects the States are
to be considered in their political capacity, and in
others as districts of individual citizens, the two
ideas embraced on different sides, instead of being
opposed to each other, ought to be combined; that
in *one* branch the *people* ought to be represented, in
the *other* the *States*."[12]

My purpose is not to single out Johnson or the
three delegates from Connecticut, as the only ones
in the Convention who recognized the difficulty of
preserving the states or suggested the equality of
state representation in the Senate. The quotations
given above I have chosen because they so clearly
point to the critical question in the organization of
the new system.

If you bear in mind the whole problem of imperial organization, from the time when the Albany
Plan was drafted, on through the Revolution and
the tribulations of the Confederate period, you find

[12] June 29.

the moment, when the Connecticut statesman made his declaration, a moment of unusual and effective drama. "Very well," he seems to say, "we have gone far, we are willing, most of us, to establish a real government; but you have not solved the problem unless you find means to protect and preserve the states." That most critical question remained.

The suggestion of solving the problem by granting equal representation of states in the Senate was adopted, partly because of a belief that with the instrument of an equal vote the states could defend themselves and ward off encroachments upon their reserved rights. And here is the amazing and amusing fact: at a later time the Convention gave up what was apparently the central idea of this famous compromise; the senators were to be allowed to vote per capita, and not by states. Furthermore, the Senate did not prove to be in the succeeding decades the particular guardian of the states' rights. So that solution of the peculiarly difficult problem was far from satisfactory. We certainly cannot say that the Senate has preserved the essentials of federalism and prevented the gradual establishment of a consolidated system. If the makers of the Constitution could have foreseen the formation of national parties, which were of national scope and which gathered together similar economic and social interests from one end of the continent to the other, they might have appreciated how helpless the Senate would be in protecting the states as corporate entities.

If this equality of state representation in the Senate was not a satisfactory means for preserving the states, was there anything else in the Constitution better adapted to the purpose? In the first place, we may see certain very essential ideas which were announced fairly early in the history of the Convention, though those ideas were not presented as specific answers to the questions propounded by Johnson. Obviously no federal plan, calculated to keep the states and the national government within their respective spheres, could actually and practically accomplish that purpose—in other words, the essence of federalism could not be worked out and estab-

lished—unless the respective spheres were delineat-
ed with a considerable degree of accuracy and detail. But again it is a striking fact that two and a
half months had gone by before there was much discussion of what powers should be assigned to the
new government. The Committee of Detail—the
committee appointed to prepare and report a constitution conformable to the proceedings of the Convention—received from the Convention for the basis
of the committee's work twenty-three resolutions,
one of which declared, "That the National Legislature ought to possess the legislative rights vested in
Congress by the Confederation; and, moreover, to
legislate in all cases for the general interests of the
Union, and also in those to which the States are
separately incompetent, or in which the harmony
of the United States may be interrupted by the exercise of individual legislation." These were admirable
indications of what should be the powers of a central
government in a federal state; the framers here laid
down the general principles upon which powers
should be distributed; but the words were indefinite
and gave no assurance that the states' sphere of sovereignty would not be gradually encroached upon.
Eleven days later (August 6), however, the committee did a momentous thing; reporting to the Convention a draft of a constitution, they enumerated,
in a series of eighteen distinct paragraphs, the powers assigned to Congress. That, in fact, was the
most satisfying answer to the critical problem of
granting adequate authority to the central government without destroying the states. The states were
safe in their own domain as long as the national government should exercise only the powers explicitly
or implicitly granted to it; the states, as part of the
federal system, were given substantial security by the
enumeration of the powers.[13] Combined with the
principle that the Constitution is law, the designa-
tion of powers granted to the central government

[13] The fear that the central government would seize upon powers
not granted was manifest in the state conventions which were called
to ratify the Constitution, and this fear caused the adoption of the
first ten amendments and especially the tenth. This danger of con-
solidation was one of the main grounds for objection to the doctrine of implied powers, the doctrine put forth by Hamilton in his
defence of the Bank Bill (1791), and it partly explains the Virginia
and Kentucky resolutions of 1798-9.

marks out the essentials of federalism established on a legal foundation.

In these later days when the generally accepted theory seems to be abroad that the national government has the right and duty to do what it may feel inclined to do, when states and their citizens are prepared to hand over any and every job they are too indolent to undertake themselves, when people seem to have accepted the notion that, if they can get the government at Washington to do things, their own hands are freed and nobody will have to pay the expense of doing them, it may be worthwhile to turn to a copy of the Constitution, read Article I, Sec. 8, and there see the list of powers assigned to Congress.

These lectures have, I hope, made reasonably clear the development of certain principles. Our constitutional system can scarcely be understood without some appreciation of the old philosophy which assumed the existence of men before government, of personal rights which are not supposed to be granted by government, of the right and the power of men to organize a political system and establish government. With this philosophy was associated the belief that by conscious agreement individuals could compact themselves into a body; and with it was associated the primary and pivotal doctrine of the American Revolution, that only a government constitutionally limited can be the government of a free people. This principle of limited government found distinct embodiment in state constitutions and in their bills of rights; and, without the principle, American federalism as a system of political organization could not have been established. Governments within a federal system must be confined each within its own sphere by law. Without the principle that a government has no inherent but only derived powers, it is difficult to see how the federal Union could have been formed; and if we adopt the theory of the British statesmen of the Revolution, to the effect that government must have all power or none, then, again, the kind of federalism embodied in the American system is impossible.

Personally, I feel strongly the necessity of preserving the essentials of federalism, the maintenance of the states, the sense of responsibility which the states should cherish if the nature of our Constitution is to be conserved. This opinion can be held not because of any thoughtless loyalty to the doctrines of the Fathers, but because of a firm belief that democracy itself, the very success of the effort to establish and maintain popular government, must find its foundation in the appreciation of responsibility. And while it seems rather absurd to summon for the defense of states' rights under the Constitution the old theory some of us learned as schoolboys—the theory and belief in the practical and, indeed, moral efficacy of local self-government—many of us still believe in its essential value. No one may be able, perhaps, to think of a state as large as New York exemplifying local self-government; it is so large that the old virtues and effects of the New England town-meeting appear quite inapplicable. And yet New York as a state has its problems, in which the nation as a whole may have no immediate and direct interest; and here is the pivotal fact: large and populous as a state may be, the people are able, if they will, to think about governmental duties and their own immediate responsibilities as they cannot think of the obligations and bureaucratic activities at Washington. When all is said, the hope for successful popular government—and in very fact its justification—is based upon the willingness of people to think.[14] In a nation of 125 millions, despite the services of newspapers, the telegraph, and the radio, there is some absurdity in accepting the notion that the people of Arizona or Montana or Georgia can direct the local concerns of a state one thousand and more miles away, or that the people thus separated and having their own problems can wisely subject all their affairs to one central governmental authority. At all events the work done by generations long gone by deserves respect; and though we cannot believe that institutions remain unaltered with the passing centuries, the achieve-

[14] It was Montesquieu, I believe, who said that in a free state it is not a matter of supreme consequence whether men think as a rule rightly or wrongly; the important thing is that they think. Without thought popular government is a delusion; and if popular government forces men to think, it needs no other defence.

ments of the past deserve study, for they throw light to our feet. One thing appears to be certain: individual liberty, law, limited government, federalism, local and personal responsibility and power—all these cannot continue unless supported by intelligence and by some portion of that earnestness and consecration which established our constitutional principles and enabled America to survive.

I have spoken much of law and of institutional forms, of the mechanisms which help to bind the Union together, but cannot close without pointing out that a nation, if it be a nation, must have in its possession certain common beliefs and principles. About seventy-one years ago, Abraham Lincoln, on his way to Washington, made a brief but signally significant though extemporaneous speech at Philadelphia. He declared the Union had been held together by the principles of the Declaration of Independence, those principles which promised the blessings of liberty to all mankind. The compelling central thought, then, is this: the nation is held together as a living thing not by courts or armies or congresses, but by an ethical principle of justice. Without it the nation, the American nation at least, would be without the very essence of nationalism. I wonder if it is necessary in these days to emphasize the need of social ethics as the heart of a vital community, a community that would really live and be a community in more than outward seeming.

But there is one thing more. These lectures have dealt largely with the principle that governments must be responsible to people—must be obedient to law; the long course of history seems to find its culmination in the establishment of the American constitutional system which is calculated to keep the government on the leash and to protect individual rights. The problem now seems to be the reverse of the old. Is it possible to conserve popular government or social order unless the people are prepared to obey government, a government which is theoretically their own creature? Are we to see a reversal of the older historical process and find that the road to liberty is the road of obedience and responsibility?

Index

160